What's Cooking at the Cooper Clinic

Our Best Recipes for your Best Health

*From the Nutrition Department
of the Cooper Clinic*

Printed by Jumbo Jack's Cookbooks
P.O. Box 247
Audubon, Iowa 50025
1-712-563-2635 or 1-800-798-2635

First Printing June 1992

Second Printing September 1992

Third Printing February 1993

ISBN 0-9633862-0-4

Order blanks are included in back of book for your convenience.

DEDICATION

To our moms...

who instilled in us the importance of providing meals for our families that were wonderfully delicious, creating fond memories of times past, and

To our many patients...

who challenged us to adapt these recipes for delicious and healthy eating.

From left to right: Cindy Kleckner, R.D., Brenda Reeves Mack, Georgia Kostas, M.P.H., R.D., Kathryn Miller, M.S., R.D., Cindy Wachtler, R.D., Patty Kirk, R.D., Veronica Coronado. Not pictured: Susan Smith.

ACKNOWLEDGEMENT

The Nutrition Department of the Cooper Clinic proudly presents **WHAT'S COOKING AT THE COOPER CLINIC**...our collection of healthy, scrumptious recipes!

Many thanks to the entire Nutrition Department for their dedication, time and talent in developing this cookbook over the past two years. Everyone's personal and professional commitment to a healthy lifestyle made this major endeavor possible. Each recipe has been tested, revised and re-tested to assure "great taste!"

Special thanks to all the wonderful staff members who contributed their best: Cindy Kleckner, R.D., Patty Kirk, R.D., Cindy Wachtler, R.D., Kathryn Miller, M.S., R.D., Brenda Reeves Mack, and Susan Smith.

To you, our readers, we hope you enjoy our "en-light-ened" dishes!

Our best recipes for your best health!

Bon Appetit!

Georgia Kostas, M.P.H., R.D.
Director-Nutrition Department
Cooper Clinic, Dallas, Texas

Veronica Coronado
Cookbook Coordinator
Cooper Clinic, Dallas, Texas

IV

FOREWORD

Proper diet is the foundation upon which physical and emotional well-being is based. I like to think of food as human fuel. Without the right kind of fuel, we lack the energy to perform at peak levels -- in intellectual, psychological and spiritual pursuits as well as physical fitness and health.

My personal mission when I started The Cooper Aerobics Center in 1970 was to encourage and support as many people as I possibly could to live longer, healthier lives through preventive medicine. The main ingredients of total well-being are regular exercise, emotional balance, and proper nutrition.

Healthful eating habits can be achieved without hardship and deprivation. The recipes in this book prove my point. Although they have been modified to reduce fat, salt and cholesterol -- ingredients that most Americans consume in excess -- they are tempting, tasty, and satisfying. I hope you and your family will enjoy them and be inspired to add the principles of good nutrition to your lifestyle.

Kenneth H. Cooper, M.D., M.P.H.
President and Founder, Cooper Clinic

THE COOPER CLINIC
AND ITS NUTRITION DEPARTMENT

The internationally known Cooper Clinic provides the most up-to-date preventive medicine expertise in the world. Thousands of private and corporate patients come through the Clinic each year to receive comprehensive, detailed medical evaluations and lifestyle enhancement guidelines.

The Cooper Clinic Nutrition Department's registered dietitians consult with each patient, adding their evaluation and nutrition prescription to diagnoses made by nine Clinic physicians whose specialties include cardiology, internal medicine, preventive medicine, radiology, cardiac rehabilitation, osteoporosis, and cholesterol and hypertension management. Nutritional balance is recognized as a key ingredient in every patient's ability to enjoy good health and total well-being.

The Nutrition Department specializes in weight management, cardiovascular health, sports nutrition and preventive medicine counseling. The staff provides individualized diet consultation, computerized diet analyses, weight-control classes, seminars, corporate lectures and children's/teen's programs. Many of the services and products associated with these programs are available by mail. These include:

* **3-day Computerized Diet Analysis** - A nutritional profile which analyzes 26 nutrients in your diet and provides nutritional recommendations.
* **Computerized Recipe Analysis** - Analyze your favorite recipe.
* **Publications:**
  * **THE BALANCING ACT FOR WEIGHT CONTROL**, by Georgia Kostas, M. P. H., R. D. and Kim Rojohn, R. D. - An easy-to-follow, step-by-step complete guide to optimal health, fitness, and weight loss.
  * **Nutrition Tips -** A series of 11 informative brochures on topics such as Fast Foods, Fiber, Cholesterol, Eating Out, and Eating-on-the-Run.

SEE ORDER FORMS IN BACK OF THIS BOOK TO OBTAIN ANY OF THE ABOVE SERVICES OR PRODUCTS

ABOUT THE NUTRIENT ANALYSIS

The analysis of each recipe in **WHAT'S COOKING AT THE COOPER CLINIC** was done with the Cooper Clinic's own computer software, "Cooper Clinic Nutrition and Exercise Evaluation System."

* The analysis includes all recipe ingredients, except those listed as optional.

* Where a choice of ingredients is listed, the first ingredient listed is the one used in the analysis.

* Where a range is given for an ingredient (1 to 1 1/2 cups oatmeal), the average of the two amounts is used (i.e., 1 1/4 cups).

* When a marinade is used, 25% of the marinade ingredients are included in the analysis. If the product is marinated and basted, 33% of the marinade is included.

* Spaghetti and rice are cooked according to package directions, but without salt and fat.

All recipes have been modified to decrease fat, cholesterol, and sodium. For those individuals with hypertension, further modification can be made by deleting salt and using unsalted products when available.

As many new fat-free products emerge on the market, we encourage you to experiment with these products if further fat reduction is desired.

Suggested Menus

<u>Weekend Brunch</u>

Raspberry Fizzle 191 cal, 2 gm fat
Ham and Egg Casserole 161 cal, 5 gm fat
Seasonal Fruit Salad 39 cal, 0 gm fat
Refrigerator Bran Muffins 155 cal, 4 gm fat

Total - 546 cal, 11 gm fat

<u>Lunch with Friends</u>

Corn Chowder 115 cal, 1 gm fat
Chicken Grape Salad 212 cal, 9 gm fat
Strawberry Romaine Salad 59 cal, 3 gm fat
Marvelous Oatmeal Muffins 111 cal, 3 gm fat

Total - 497 cal, 16 gm fat

<u>Entertaining for Dinner</u>

Marinated Pork Tenderloin 148 cal, 5 gm fat
Garlic Roasted Potatoes 134 cal, 5 gm fat
Peppered Romaine Salad 63 cal, 5 gm fat
Light Angel Biscuits 110 cal, 3 gm fat
Fruited Angel Ice 124 cal, 0 gm fat

Total - 579 cal, 18 gm fat

Picnic in the Park

Southern Fried Chicken 185 cal, 5 gm fat
New Potato Salad with
Mustard Vinaigrette 153 cal, 5 gm fat
Coleslaw 97 cal, 5 gm fat
Oatmeal Raspberry Bars 134 cal, 4 gm fat

Total - 569 cal, 19 gm fat

Mexican Fiesta

Gazpacho 46 cal, 1 gm fat
Enchiladas Suisas (2 enchiladas) 404 cal, 14 gm fat
Spanish Rice 113 cal, 4 gm fat
South of the Border Chips (6 chips) 86 cal, 2 gm fat
Mango Tomato Salsa 16 cal, 0 fat

Total - 665 cal, 21 gm fat

A Special Shower

Apple-Pineapple Slush 57 cal, 0 gm fat
Cucumber Sandwiches (2 pcs) 106 cal, 4 gm fat
Dipped Fruit (4 pcs) 89 cal, 3 gm fat
Celery Stuffed with Shrimp (2 pcs) 28 cal, 2 gm fat
Mini Fruit Pizzas 161 cal, 4 gm fat

Total - 441 cal, 13 gm fat

All menus above contain less than 30% calories from fat.

Our Standard Abbreviations

tsp.	-	teaspoon	**sm.** -	small
T.	-	tablespoon	**med.** -	medium
c.	-	cup	**lg.** -	large
oz.	-	ounce or ounces	**pt.** -	pint
lb.	-	pound or pounds	**qt.** -	quart
sq.	-	square	**pk.** -	peck
doz.	-	dozen	**bu.** -	bushel
ctn.	-	carton or container	**env.** -	envelope(s)
pkg.	-	package(s)	**gm.** -	gram(s)
btl.	-	bottle	**cal.** -	calories
pkt.	-	packet(s)	**mg.** -	milligram(s)

Table of Contents

FAVORITE RECIPES

Recipe Name	Page Number

Sip
It

Sip It

Sip It

Fruit Smoothy

Nutrition Staff

1 (8 oz.) can fruit cocktail,
   packed in its own juice
1 c. skim milk
1/4 c. nonfat dry powdered
   milk

1/4 c. plain nonfat yogurt
1/2 tsp. vanilla
1/2 c. (3-4 lg.) ice cubes
Cinnamon, to taste

1. In a blender container, combine undrained fruit cocktail, and remaining ingredients except ice cubes.
2. Cover; blend until combined.
3. Add ice cubes; cover and blend until smooth.
4. Sprinkle with cinnamon.
5. Serve immediately.

Yield: 4 servings
Per Serving (1 cup):
   78 cal, 0 gm fat, 6 gm pro, 13 gm carb, 3 mg chol, 85 mg sodium, 1 gm dietary fiber

Pinana Frost

Cindy Kleckner, R.D.

1 c. skim milk
1 c. banana, sliced
   (approx. 2 bananas)

3 T. frozen pineapple juice
   concentrate, undiluted
1/4 tsp. vanilla

1. In blender container, combine all ingredients.
2. Cover; blend until smooth.
3. Serve immediately.

Yield: 2 servings
Per Serving (1 cup):
   204 cal, 1 gm fat, 6 gm pro, 46 gm carb, 2 mg chol, 64 mg sodium, 2 gm dietary fiber

Strawberry Delight

Cindy Kleckner, R.D.

1 c. skim milk	1 T. sugar
1/2 c. strawberries, sliced	1/4 tsp. vanilla

1. In a blender container, combine milk, strawberries, sugar and vanilla.
2. Cover and blend on high speed until strawberries are puréed.
3. Garnish with whole strawberry.

Yield: 1 serving
Per Serving:
   161 cal, 1 gm fat, 9 gm pro, 30 gm carb, 4 mg chol, 126 mg sodium,
   2 gm dietary fiber

Orange Frost

Cindy Kleckner, R.D

1 1/2 c. orange sherbet	4 ice cubes
1 (6 oz.) can frozen orange	1 c. ice water
juice concentrate,	3 (12 oz.) cans sugar-free
undiluted	lemon lime soft drink

1. In a blender container, combine all the ingredients except soft drink.
2. Cover; blend until smooth.
3. Pour into 8 glasses.
4. Pour soft drink into sides of glasses; stir gently.

Yield: 8 servings
Per Serving (1 cup):
   93 cal, 1 gm fat, 1 gm pro, 21 gm carb, 3 mg chol, 39 mg sodium, 0 gm
   dietary fiber

For strong bones, you need 2 to 3
nonfat dairy products daily.

Very Fruity Frozen Frappé

Cindy Kleckner, R.D.

1 c. plain nonfat yogurt
1 banana, frozen

1 to 2 T. frozen fruit juice
  concentrate, undiluted
1/8 tsp. vanilla

1. In a blender container, combine all ingredients.
2. Cover and blend on high speed until smooth.
3. Serve immediately.

NOTE: To freeze ripe bananas, remove peel, cut into quarters, and seal in an airtight freezer container.

Yield: 1 serving
Per Serving:
  276 cal, 1 gm fat, 15 gm pro, 54 gm carb, 4 mg chol, 176 mg sodium, 2 gm dietary fiber

Fruity Milkshake

Cindy Kleckner, R.D.

1/2 c. skim milk
1 T. nonfat dry powdered
  milk

1/2 c. frozen unsweetened
  strawberries
1/2 banana
1/2 c. ice cubes

1. In a blender container, combine ingredients with ice; blend until frothy.

Yield: 1 serving
Per Serving (1 cup)
  150 cal, 1 gm fat, 8 gm pro, 30 gm carb, 3 mg chol, 105 mg sodium, 3 gm dietary fiber

Peachy Fruit Shake
Cindy Kleckner, R.D.

1 c. plain nonfat yogurt
1/2 c. skim milk

1/2 c. canned peach
halves, packed in its
own juice, drained

1. In blender container, combine all ingredients.
2. Cover and blend until smooth.
3. Pour into 2 large glasses and serve immediately.

Yield: 2 servings
Per Serving (1 cup):
100 cal, 0 gm fat, 9 gm pro, 15 gm carb, 3 mg chol, 120 mg sodium,
1 gm dietary fiber

Raspberry Fizzle
Barbara Coronado

2 c. raspberry sherbet   **2 c. orange juice**

1. Fill 4 glasses with 1/2 cup sherbet each.
2. Pour 1/2 cup orange juice over the sherbet.

Yield: 4 servings
Per Serving:
191 cal, 2 gm fat, 2 gm pro, 43 carb, 7 mg chol, 45 mg sodium, 0 gm
dietary fiber

*Low-fat and nonfat yogurts are excellent sources of calcium
and contain 300 to 400 mg of calcium per 1 cup serving.*

Apple Pineapple Slush
Susan Smith

1 (46 oz.) can pineapple
    juice
1 (46 oz.) can apple juice

1 (2-liter) btl. Diet Sprite or
    Diet 7-Up
Orange slices & long-
    stemmed cherries (optional)

1. In a large container, combine juices. Freeze.
2. Remove from freezer about 3 hours before serving. If still frozen, break
   up. Should be slush consistency.
3. Add Diet Sprite or Diet 7-Up and mix.
4. Garnish with orange slices and long-stemmed cherries.

Yield: 26
Per Serving (3/4 cup without garnish):
    57 cal, 0 gm fat, 0 gm pro, 14 gm carb, 0 mg chol, 13 mg sodium, 0 gm
    dietary fiber

Frozen Banana Punch
Susan Smith

1 (46 oz.) can pineapple
    juice
1 (6 oz.) can frozen orange
    juice concentrate
1 (6 oz.) can frozen
    lemonade concentrate

5 ripe bananas
6 c. water
3 liters diet ginger ale

1. In a large container, combine juices.
2. Using a blender, purée bananas with water. Add mixture to juices after
   thoroughly blending.
3. Freeze in a large container.
4. Before serving, thaw for about 3 hours or until punch base is slushy.
   Add ginger ale.

Yield: 34
Per Serving (3/4 cup):
    59 cal, 0 gm fat, 1 gm pro, 15 gm carb, 0 mg chol, 15 mg sodium, 0 gm
    dietary fiber

Cranapple Warmer

Veronica Coronado

2 qt. apple cider
2 qt. cranberry juice cock-
    tail, low-calorie
1/4 c. brown sugar

4 cinnamon sticks or 1 tsp.
    cinnamon
8 cloves or 1/4 tsp. ground
    cloves

1. Combine all ingredients.
2. Simmer on low in crockpot or on stove for 2 hours; serve warm.

Yield: 16 servings
Per Serving (1 cup):
    98 cal, 0 gm fat, 0 gm pro, 24 gm carb, 0 mg chol, 6 gm sodium, 0 gm
    dietary fiber

Lemonade and Tea Cooler

Veronica Coronado

8 tea bags, decaffeinated
3 qt. boiling water
1 (32 oz.) btl. diet ginger
    ale, chilled

1 (12 oz.) can lemonade
    concentrate
Lemon slices (optional)
Mint for garnish (optional)

1. Place tea bags in boiling water and steep 10 minutes; remove tea
    bags.
2. Add lemonade; chill.
3. Just before serving, add ginger ale and pour over ice or serve as
    punch.
4. Garnish with lemon slice and sprig of mint.

Yield: 17 servings
Per Serving (1 cup):
    41 cal, 0 gm fat, 0 gm pro, 12 gm carb, 0 mg chol, 9 mg sodium, 0 gm
    dietary fiber

Lemon Almond Iced Tea

Veronica Coronado

2 c. water
4 tea bags, decaffeinated
2 c. cold water
1 (12 oz.) can frozen lemonade concentrate, thawed

2 tsp. vanilla
2 tsp. almond extract
2 qt. cold water

1. Bring 2 cups water to a boil.
2. Add tea bags and steep 5 minutes.
3. Add 2 cups cold water, lemonade, vanilla and almond extracts.
4. When ready to serve, add 2 quarts water; serve over ice.

Yields 14 servings
Per Serving (1 cup):
   52 cal, 0 gm fat, 0 gm pro, 14 gm carb, 0 mg chol, 0 mg sodium, 0 gm
   dietary fiber

Mocktail

Harriet Guthrie

1 (46 oz.) can V-8 juice,
   chilled
1 (1 liter) btl. club soda,
   chilled

2 T. lemon juice
1 lemon, sliced (optional)

1. Combine all ingredients except sliced lemon.
2. Pour into glasses; add ice cubes and garnish with lemon slices.

Yield: 10 servings
Per Serving (1 cup):
   42 cal, 0 gm fat, 1 gm pro, 9 gm carb, 0 mg chol, 686 mg sodium, 1 gm
   dietary fiber

Notes and Recipes

_____

_____

_____

_____

_____

_____

_____

_____

_____

_____

_____

_____

_____

Awesome
Appetizers
&
Souper
Soups

Awesome Appetizers & Souper Soups

Awesome Appetizers & Souper Soups

Celery Stuffed with Shrimp

Cindy Wachtler, R.D.

4 oz. cooked, shelled & chopped salad shrimp
1/3 c. light Miracle Whip
1/4 c. unsweetened crushed pineapple, drained
1 1/2 tsp. lemon juice
1 1/2 tsp. onion, finely chopped
2 tsp. fresh parsley, minced
Dash of hot sauce
8 (8-inch) stalks celery

1. Combine all ingredients except celery; chill.
2. Cut celery crosswise into 2-inch pieces.
3. Stuff mixture into celery pieces.

Yield: 32 pieces
Per Serving (1 piece):
14 cal, 1 gm fat, 1 gm pro, 1 gm carb, 6 mg chol, 25 mg sodium, 0 gm dietary fiber

One ounce of most frozen yogurt contains 20-36 calories per ounce compared to 70 calories per ounce in premium ice creams.

Pepper Stuffed Mushrooms

Sandi Hanson

24 lg. mushrooms
1 tsp. olive oil
1/4 c. onion, chopped
1 clove garlic, minced
1/2 c. green bell pepper,
    chopped
1/2 tsp. salt

1/4 tsp. pepper
3 T. Parmesan cheese
3 T. capers, chopped
1 T. bread crumbs
Nonstick vegetable
    cooking spray

1. Wash mushrooms; remove stems and chop stems.
2. In olive oil sauté mushroom stems, onion, garlic and green pepper for 5 minutes.
3. Add salt, pepper, Parmesan cheese, capers and bread crumbs; stuff mushrooms.
4. Place in baking dish sprayed with cooking spray.
5. Bake at 375°F. for 15 minutes; serve warm.

Yield: 6 servings
Per Serving (4 mushrooms):
     47 cal, 2 gm fat, 3 gm pro, 5 gm carb, 2 mg chol, 245 mg sodium, 2 gm dietary fiber

Skinny Nachos

Cindy Kleckner, R.D.

1 soft corn tortilla
Seasoning i.e., Bakon's
    cheddar cheese, cayenne
    pepper, or your favorite

1 oz. part-skim mozzarella
    cheese, shredded

1. Preheat oven to 350°F.
2. Cut corn tortilla into 8 triangular "pie" slices.
3. Add seasonings of choice to chips; bake on cookie sheet for 15 minutes.
4. Sprinkle cheese over crispy chips; broil until cheese is bubbly.

Yield: 1 serving
Per Serving:
     147 cal, 6 gm fat, 10 gm pro, 14 gm carb, 16 mg chol, 205 mg sodium, 2 gm dietary fiber

Mini-Melba Pizzas
Patty Kirk, R.D.

1/2 c. spaghetti sauce
24 wholegrain melba toast
   rounds
6 med. fresh mushrooms,
   thinly sliced

3 green onions, sliced
6 T. part-skim mozzarella
   cheese, shredded
2 T. low-fat Cheddar
   cheese, shredded

1. Place melba toast rounds on a baking sheet.
2. Spread 1 teaspoon spaghetti sauce on each round.
3. Evenly distribute mushrooms, onions and cheeses on top of spaghetti sauce on each round.
4. Preheat oven to 400°F.
5. Bake for 3 minutes or until cheeses melt.

Yield: 24 servings
Per Serving (1 pizza):
   21 cal, 1 gm fat, 1 gm pro, 2 gm carb, 1 mg chol, 37 mg sodium, 0 gm dietary fiber

Cucumber Sandwiches
Susan Smith

1 (12 oz.) ctn. low-fat
   cream cheese
1 pkg. Good Seasons Italian
   salad dressing mix
1 lg. cucumber, peeled &
   grated

1/4 med. onion, chopped
1 lg. loaf thin-sliced wheat
   bread (24 slices)

1. Blend cream cheese, salad dressing mix, grated cucumber and onion.
2. Chill in refrigerator for 1 hour.
3. Spread mixture on bread, being careful not to spread to the edges.
4. Cut off crusts after filling sandwiches.
5. Place dampened paper towel in bottom of plastic container as well as on top of sandwiches and store overnight or all day.
6. Cut sandwiches into fourths before serving.

Yield: 48 sandwiches
Per Serving (1 mini sandwich):
   53 cal, 2 gm fat, 2 gm pro, 6 gm carb, 6 mg chol, 93 mg sodium, 0 gm dietary fiber

Pita Crackers
Nutrition Staff

4 wholewheat pita
pockets

Nonstick vegetable
cooking spray

1. Preheat oven to 300°F. Spray baking sheet with cooking spray.
2. Cut pita pockets into quarters; split each apart.
3. Place wedges on prepared baking sheet.
4. Bake 10 minutes, or until well toasted; cool.
5. Crackers can be stored in an airtight container.

Yield: 32 crackers
Per Serving (1 cracker):
21 cal, 0 gm fat, 1 gm pro, 4 gm carb, 0 mg chol, 42 mg sodium, 1 gm
dietary fiber

Festive Spinach Dip
Cindy Wachtler, R.D.

1 (12 oz.) ctn. low-fat
cottage cheese
1 (10 oz.) box frozen chop-
ped spinach, thawed
& drained
1/2 c. light sour cream

1/4 c. dry vegetable soup
mix
3 tsp. onion, grated
1 tsp. lemon juice
1 (8 oz.) can chopped water
chestnuts, drained

1. Position knife blade in food processor bowl; add cottage cheese.
2. Process until smooth, scraping sides of processor bowl once; place in
a medium bowl, and set aside.
3. Squeeze excess water from spinach.
4. Add spinach and remaining ingredients to cheese mixture; stir well.
5. Cover and refrigerate 3 hours.
6. Serve with unsalted crackers, bread sticks, or raw vegetables.

Yield: 3 cups (48 tablespoons)
Per Serving (1 tablespoon):
13 cal, <1 gm fat, 1 gm pro, 2 gm carb, 1 mg chol, 63 mg sodium, 0 gm
dietary fiber

Vegetable Dip

Nutrition Staff

1 1/2 c. low-fat cottage cheese
1/2 c. plain nonfat yogurt

1/2 tsp. worcestershire sauce
1 (.4 oz.) pkg. dry ranch-style party dip

1. Blend together all ingredients until smooth.
2. Serve with raw vegetables. May also be used as salad dressing or over baked potatoes.

Yield: 32 servings
Per Serving (1 tablespoon):
    10 cal, <1 gm fat, 2 gm pro, 1 gm carb, 1 mg chol, 111 mg sodium, 0 gm dietary fiber

Calico Cracker Spread

Cindy Kleckner, R.D.

1/2 c. plain nonfat yogurt
1 c. low-fat cottage cheese
1/8 c. green bell pepper, chopped
1/8 c. red bell pepper, chopped

1/4 c. green onions, sliced
1/2 c. carrots, shredded
1/8 tsp. pepper

1. In a mixing bowl, combine all ingredients.
2. Refrigerate.
3. Serve with your favorite crackers.

Yield: 7 servings
Per Serving (4 tablespoons):
    37 cal, <1 gm fat, 5 gm pro, 3 gm carb, 4 mg chol, 147 mg sodium, 0 gm dietary fiber

Food labels are road maps to good nutrition.

Dipped Fruit

Karla Costello

1 (7 oz.) jar marshmallow
    creme
6 oz. low-fat cream cheese

2 apples
32 strawberries

1. Combine marshmallow creme and cream cheese and blend with mixer until well combined.
2. Slice each apple into 16 pieces.
3. Place dip in serving bowl and arrange apples and strawberries on a plate with dip.

Yield: 16 servings
Per Serving (4 pieces of fruit with 1 tablespoon dip):
    89 cal, 3 gm fat, 1 gm pro, 15 gm carb, 9 mg chol, 51 mg sodium, 1 gm dietary fiber

Low-cholesterol foods are not always low-fat.

Choose low-fat snacks of fresh fruit, melba toast, pretzels,
air-popped popcorn, graham crackers, animal crackers,
rice cakes, nonfat yogurt and mini bagels.

Yogurt Cheese

Nutrition Staff

Yogurt cheese is a nonfat cheese substitute that has the consistency of cream cheese. It is a wonderful substitute to use in place of sour cream, cream cheese, mayonnaise or ricotta cheese.

Compare the calories:

ricotta cheese (part-skim)	20 cal/T
sour cream	30 cal/T
light sour cream	20 cal/T
cream cheese	50 cal/T
low-fat cream cheese	40 cal/T
mayonnaise	100 cal/T
diet mayonnaise	50 cal/T
yogurt cheese	16 cal/T

2 c. plain nonfat yogurt   **15"x15" piece of cheese-cloth**

1. Spoon yogurt into the cheesecloth.
2. Tie the cheesecloth at the top and hang the "bag" over a bowl to catch the whey.
3. Refrigerate and allow to drain 8 to 10 hours.
4. Place in container and keep refrigerated 1 1/2 to 2 weeks. (Optional: Yogurt cheese can also be made in a coffee filter.)
5. Check the yogurt you use to make sure it does not contain a stabilizer or gelatin base or carrageenan. This yogurt will not separate well. Choose a yogurt with the culture in it.
6. If cooking with yogurt cheese, add 1 tablespoon cornstarch per 1 cup yogurt cheese. This keeps the mixture from separating.
7. Flavored yogurts may be used or add your choice of seasonings, i.e., chives, onion powder, etc.

Yield: 1 cup (16 tablespoons)
Per Serving (1 tablespoon):
16 cal, 0 gm fat, 2 gm pro, 2 gm carb, 1 mg chol, 22 mg sodium, 0 gm dietary fiber

Choose margarines with "liquid
vegetable oil" as the first ingredient.

Black-Eyed Pea Soup

Modified from the
Black-eyed Pea Restaurant

2 oz. Canadian bacon
1 c. onion, chopped
2 c. tomatoes, chopped
2 T. jalapeños, finely
   chopped (optional)
1/2 tsp. minced garlic
Pinch of salt

Dash of pepper
3 c. water
2 chicken bouillon cubes
4 (15.8 oz.) cans black-eyed peas
3 c. low-fat Cheddar
   cheese, grated
Nonstick vegetable cooking spray

1. Spray saucepan with cooking spray; add Canadian bacon, onions, tomatoes, jalapeños, garlic, salt and pepper, and cover.
2. Sauté until onions are transparent. If ingredients begin to stick you may add up to 2 tablespoons of water.
3. Add the water; dissolve the bouillon cubes in the mixture.
4. Drain juice from peas and rinse peas with water.
5. Add peas to the soup and simmer for 20 minutes or until steaming hot.
6. Add the cheese and stir until the cheese is just melted.

Yield: 12 servings
Per Serving (1 cup):
   220 cal, 6 gm fat, 17 gm pro, 25 carb, 18 mg chol, 411 mg sodium, 6 gm dietary fiber

Hearty Hamburger Soup   Harriet Guthrie

1 lb. lean ground beef
2 (15 oz.) cans ranch-style
   beans, undrained
1 (16 oz.) can tomatoes, undrained
1 (16 oz.) can Rotel tomatoes undrained (or use two
   16 oz. cans Rotel tomatoes
   for above 2 cans if
   a hotter soup is desired)

1/4 c. green bell pepper,
   diced
1 (10 oz.) pkg. frozen corn,
   thawed
1 lg. onion, diced
1 to 2 T. sweet relish
Dash of pepper

1. Brown meat in large skillet; drain fat.
2. Add rest of ingredients; simmer for 10 minutes or until hot. May simmer longer to develop spices if desired.
3. Add water if a soupier dish is desired.

Yield: 8 servings
Per Serving:
   274 cal, 9 gm fat, 19 gm pro, 32 gm carb, 37 mg chol, 601 mg sodium, 9 gm dietary fiber

Cream of Corn Soup
Cindy Kleckner, R.D.

3 T. onion, minced
2 c. frozen corn, thawed
2 1/2 T. margarine
2 T. flour

1 qt. skim milk
1/2 tsp. salt (optional)
1/2 tsp. pepper

1. In saucepan, sauté onion in 1/2 tablespoon margarine until soft.
2. Put corn through a food processor, add to onion mixture, and cook until it begins to brown; stir occasionally.
3. Add remaining margarine, and then the flour; cook slowly for 3 minutes.
4. Add milk, salt and pepper; cook until thickened and smooth.

Yield: 6 servings
Per Serving (1 cup):
159 cal, 5 gm fat, 8 gm pro, 22 gm carb, 3 mg chol, 142 mg sodium, 2 gm dietary fiber

Corn Chowder
Veronica Coronado

1/2 T. margarine
1 c. onion, chopped
2 potatoes, peeled & diced
    into bite-size pieces
1 (12 oz.) can evaporated
    skimmed milk

1 (16 1/2 oz.) can cream-
    style corn
1 tsp. salt
1/4 tsp. pepper

1. Melt margarine; cook onion in margarine until tender and transparent.
2. In a soup pot, start potatoes in 4 cups water; cook potatoes until done. Do not drain.
3. Add all remaining ingredients including onion.
4. Cook over low to medium heat for 25 to 30 minutes, stirring occasionally.

Yield: 8 servings
Per Serving (1 cup):
115 cal, 1 gm fat, 6 gm pro, 23 carb, 2 mg chol, 497 mg sodium, 2 gm dietary fiber

Minestrone Soup

Nutrition Staff

1 onion, diced
1 1/2 c. celery, chopped
1/4 c. chicken broth
1 (14 1/2 oz.) can tomatoes
    with juice
3 c. chicken broth
1/4 c. fresh parsley,
    chopped
3 c. water
Dash of pepper
2 bay leaves
1 tsp. oregano
2 tsp. basil

1/2 tsp. rosemary
1/2 tsp. minced garlic
1/2 c. carrot, chopped
1/2 c. zucchini, diced
1/2 c. potato, diced
1/4 c. green bell pepper,
    chopped
1/4 c. corn
1 c. cooked garbanzo
    beans
1 c. mushrooms, sliced
1/2 c. macaroni, dry
1/2 c. cooked barley

1. Sauté onion and celery in 1/4 cup chicken broth until soft.
2. Add the tomatoes, 3 cups chicken broth, water, parsley, seasonings and vegetables.
3. Simmer soup for 30 minutes.
4. Add macaroni, garbanzo beans and barley.
5. Continue cooking over medium heat for 10 minutes.

Yield: 8 servings
Per Serving (1 cup):
    123 cal, 2 gm fat, 7 gm pro, 21 gm carb, 0 mg chol, 429 mg sodium, 5 gm dietary fiber

Taste before you salt.

Calico Bean Chowder   Cindy Kleckner, R.D.

1/2 lb. dried navy beans or
  2 c. canned kidney
  beans
1 tsp. salt
1 c. onion, chopped
1 1/2 c. celery, chopped
1/4 c. diet margarine
1/4 c. flour

1/4 tsp. pepper
3 c. skim milk
1 (16 oz) can tomatoes
1 (10 oz.) pkg. frozen
  whole kernel corn
1 to 3 dashes Tabasco
  sauce

1. Rinse dried beans and soak in 3 cups cold water for 6 to 8 hours; DO NOT REFRIGERATE.
2. Drain, and rinse.
3. In a large stockpot, cook beans in 4 cups hot water with 1 teaspoon salt; cook until tender about 2 hours; DO NOT DRAIN.
4. Sauté onion and celery in diet margarine in saucepan; blend in flour and pepper.
5. Stir in skim milk and bring to a boil.
6. Immediately add to bean mixture (if using canned kidney beans, add them at this time), then add tomatoes with juice, corn and Tabasco sauce.
7. Heat to boiling; cook for 10 to 15 minutes and serve hot.

Yield: 12 servings
Per Serving (1 cup):
  145 cal, 2 gm fat, 8 gm pro, 24 gm carb, 1 mg chol, 338 mg sodium, 5 gm dietary fiber

To reduce a too-salty taste from soup or stew, add a cubed raw potato and heat for 10 minutes. Remember to remove the potato before serving.

Black Bean Soup
Veronica Coronado

2 c. dried black beans
5 c. water
1 onion, chopped
1 rib celery, thinly sliced
2 cloves garlic, pressed

1/4 c. fresh cilantro,
  chopped
1/8 tsp. dry mustard
1/2 tsp. salt
1/2 tsp. pepper
1/2 c. dry sherry

1. Cover beans with water and soak overnight; drain.
2. Add 5 cups water, onion, celery, garlic, cilantro, mustard, salt and pepper.
3. Bring to a boil; simmer, covered for 3 1/2 to 4 hours, or until beans are tender.
4. Add sherry the last 15 minutes of cooking.
5. Pour soup into warmed bowls.

Yield: 8 servings
Per Serving (1 cup):
  196 cal, 1 gm fat, 11 gm pro, 34 gm carb, 0 mg chol, 142 mg sodium, 3 gm dietary fiber

Tomato Bouillon
Jean Wisner, R.D.

4 c. tomato juice
2 c. chicken broth
1 T. lemon juice

1 tsp. sugar
1/2 tsp. dillweed

1. Combine all ingredients and heat thoroughly.

Yield: 8 servings
Per Serving (3/4 cup):
  33 cal, 0 gm fat, 2 gm pro, 7 gm carb, 0 mg chol, 605 mg sodium, 1 gm dietary fiber

Make It Healthy Cream Soup Mix

Cindy Kleckner, R.D.

2 c. nonfat dry powdered
   milk
3/4 c. cornstarch
1 T. instant chicken bouillon
3 T. instant chicken bouillon,
   low-sodium

2 T. onion flakes
1 tsp. thyme
1 tsp. basil
1/2 tsp. pepper

1. Combine all ingredients and mix well; store in airtight container.
2. Mix 1/3 cup with 1 1/4 cup boiling water in a saucepan as substitute for 1 can soup in casserole recipe.
3. Add mushroom, celery, or chicken to create flavor desired.

Yield: 6 servings
Per Serving (1/3 cup):
   237 cal, 1 gm fat, 16 gm pro, 41 gm carb, 8 mg chol, 734 mg sodium, 0 gm dietary fiber

Notes and Recipes

_____

_____

_____

_____

_____

_____

_____

_____

_____

_____

_____

_____

_____

Tossed Temptations & Delightful Dressings

Tossed Temptations & Delightful Dressings

Tossed Temptations & Delightful Dressings

Peppered Romaine Salad

Jean Wisner, R.D.

1/2 tsp. minced garlic
2 T. olive oil
3 T. red wine vinegar
1 T. orange juice
2 T. minced onion
2 T. tomato, peeled, seeded & chopped

1 sm. jalapeño pepper, seeded & finely chopped
3 c. romaine lettuce
3 c. Belgian endive
1 red bell pepper, cut into strips
1 yellow bell pepper, cut into strips

1. Combine garlic and oil in a small bowl; let stand 30 minutes.
2. Add vinegar and next 4 ingredients; stir well and set aside.
3. Line 6 salad plates with romaine lettuce leaves.
4. Tear remaining romaine and endive into small pieces; add pepper.
5. Drizzle each with 1 1/2 tablespoons vinegar mixture.

Yield: 6 servings
Per Serving:
63 cal, 5 gm fat, 1 gm pro, 5 gm carb, 0 mg chol, 23 mg sodium, 1 gm dietary fiber

*For quick salads, wash and tear greens
and store in an airtight container.*

Chef's Salad

Nutrition Staff

1/2 c. radishes, sliced
1/4 c. green onions, sliced
1/2 c. cauliflower florets,
  thinly sliced
2 T. salad dressing, low-
  calorie

2 c. salad greens, torn into
  bite-size pieces
1 oz. low-fat cheese, cut
  into julienne strips
2 oz. turkey breast, cut
  into julienne strips
4 cherry tomatoes, halved

1. In a large bowl, combine radishes, green onions and cauliflower with salad dressing; toss.
2. Refrigerate 4 hours, tossing occasionally.
3. Place salad greens in 2 individual salad bowls.
4. Spoon 1/2 of the vegetable mixture on top of each bowl of greens.
5. Arrange cheese, turkey and cherry tomatoes on top of greens.

Yield: 2 servings
Per Serving:
    133 cal, 4 gm fat, 14 gm pro, 10 gm carb, 33 mg chol, 240 mg sodium, 3 gm dietary fiber

Greek Spinach Salad

Jean Wisner, R.D.

1 (10 oz.) box frozen
  artichokes, thawed
1 lb. spinach, cleaned
3 green onions, thinly sliced
1 sm. cucumber, sliced
1 hard-cooked egg white, sliced
5 or 6 cherry tomatoes, halved

8 oz. fresh mushrooms,
  sliced
2 oz. feta cheese,
  crumbled
2 T. (about 5) sliced ripe olives
1/3 c. fat-free Italian
  dressing

1. Thaw artichokes in microwave on defrost for 5 minutes.
2. Break spinach leaves in bite-size pieces.
3. Place spinach in a bowl and mix with onion and cucumber.
4. On top of spinach, arrange rows of egg white, artichoke hearts, cherry tomatoes and mushrooms.
5. Sprinkle with cheese and olives.
6. Pour dressing over salad and toss lightly.

Yield: 6 servings
Per Serving:
    91 cal, 3 gm fat, 6 gm pro, 11 gm carb, 8 mg chol, 414 mg sodium, 4 gm dietary fiber

Salada Guadalajara
Jean Wisner, R.D.

1/4 c. plain nonfat yogurt
1/4 c. low-fat mayonnaise
1/4 c. light sour cream
1/4 c. chili sauce
1 tsp. salsa
1/4 tsp. ground cumin
1/2 tsp. minced garlic
1 tsp. onion, finely minced
1/4 tsp. salt

1/4 tsp. pepper
14 c. romaine lettuce, torn
1/2 med. green bell pepper,
    seeded & cut into strips
1/3 c. green onions, sliced
1 (9 oz.) can red kidney
    beans, rinsed & drained
2 hard-cooked egg whites,
    chopped

1. In a small bowl, combine yogurt, mayonnaise, sour cream, chili sauce, salsa, cumin, garlic, onion, salt and pepper; cover and chill overnight.
2. Just before serving, combine the salad greens, green pepper, green onions and kidney beans in a salad bowl.
3. Add dressing and toss to coat greens evenly.
4. Sprinkle top with chopped egg whites.

Yield: 8 servings
Per Serving:
    97 cal, 3 gm fat, 5 gm pro, 12 gm carb, 1 mg chol, 292 mg sodium, 3 gm dietary fiber

Strawberry-Romaine Salad
Veronica Coronado

3 1/2 c. torn romaine
    lettuce, tightly packed
1 c. trimmed watercress,
    tightly packed
1 c. fresh strawberries, sliced
1/2 c. celery, sliced
1 T. sliced almonds, toasted

1/4 c. Strawberry Vinegar
    (See Index)
1 1/2 tsp. oil
1/4 tsp. salt
1/4 tsp. sugar
1/4 tsp. pepper
1/8 tsp. celery seed (optional)

1. Combine first 5 ingredients in a large bowl; toss gently.
2. Combine Strawberry Vinegar and next 4 ingredients; stir well.
3. Pour dressing over lettuce mixture; toss well.

Yield: 4 servings
Per Serving:
    59 cal, 3 gm fat, 2 gm pro, 7 gm carb, 0 mg chol, 154 mg sodium, 3 gm dietary fiber

Strawberry Spinach Salad   Brenda Mack

1 lb. asparagus spears
4 c. fresh spinach, torn into
   bite-size pieces
4 c. red leaf lettuce, torn
   into bite-size pieces

1 c. fresh strawberries,
   sliced
1 c. fresh blueberries
3/4 lb. cooked turkey, cut
   into 1/2" cubes
2 T. pecans, chopped

DRESSING:
1/4 c. Strawberry Vinegar
   (See Index)
1 1/2 tsp. vegetable oil

1/4 tsp. sugar
1/4 tsp. salt
1/4 tsp. pepper

1. Snap off and discard woody bases from asparagus.
2. Cut into 1-inch pieces.
3. Place asparagus in a 1-quart microwave-safe baking dish with 2 tablespoons water; cook, covered on full power (high) for 5 to 7 minutes or until just crisp-tender, stirring once.
4. Drain asparagus; rinse with cold water.
5. Let stand in cold water until cool; drain.
6. Combine dressing ingredients; set aside.
7. In a salad bowl, combine asparagus, greens, berries and turkey; add dressing mixture and toss.
8. Top with pecans.

Yield: 4 servings
Per Serving:
   261 cal, 9 gm fat, 30 gm pro, 17 gm carb, 65 mg chol, 249 sodium, 6 gm dietary fiber

It is easier to MAINTAIN good health through
proper exercise, diet and emotional balance
than it is to REGAIN it once it is lost.

Strawberry-Grapefruit Spinach Salad

Jean Wisner, R.D.

3 T. red wine vinegar
2 T. apple juice concentrate
2 T. vegetable oil
1/4 tsp. grapefruit rind, grated
1/4 tsp. poppy seeds

1/8 tsp. dry mustard
2 c. grapefruit sections (about 2 med. grapefruit)
2 c. strawberries, halved
1/2 lb. spinach, torn in bite-size pieces

1. Combine first 6 ingredients in a jar; cover tightly and shake vigorously.
2. Chill 3 hours.
3. Combine grapefruit, strawberries and spinach in a large bowl; add dressing, tossing gently to coat.

Yield: 8 servings
Per Serving:
77 cal, 4 gm fat, 1 gm pro, 11 gm carb, 0 mg chol, 23 mg sodium, 2 gm dietary fiber

Orange Salad with Honey Vinaigrette

Jean Wisner, R.D.

3 T. white wine vinegar
2 T. water
2 T. vegetable oil
2 T. honey
4 c. red leaf lettuce, torn into small pieces

4 c. romaine lettuce, torn into small pieces
4 med. oranges, seedless, peeled & sliced crosswise
1 sm. purple onion, sliced & separated into rings

1. Combine wine vinegar, water, oil and honey in a jar; cover tightly and shake vigorously and set aside.
2. Place 1/2 cup of each lettuce on a salad plate; top with oranges and onion slices.
3. Drizzle each with 1 tablespoon dressing.

Yield: 8 servings
Per Serving:
93 cal, 4 gm fat, 2 gm pro, 14 gm carb, 0 mg chol, 4 mg sodium, 3 gm dietary fiber

Tomato Basil Salad

Nutrition Staff

2 tomatoes, thinly sliced
8 yellow tomatoes, thinly
　sliced
2 plum tomatoes, chopped

8 fresh basil leaves
3 tsp. olive oil
Pepper, to taste

1.　Arrange tomato slices on 4 salad plates. Top with chopped plum tomatoes and basil leaves.
2.　Sprinkle each plate with 3/4 teaspoon olive oil and a generous dash of pepper.

Yield: 4 servings
Per Serving:
　　99 cal, 4 gm fat, 3 gm pro, 15 gm carb, 0 mg chol, 28 mg sodium, 4 gm dietary fiber

Colorful Rice Salad

Jean Wisner, R.D.

1 (10 oz.) pkg. frozen
　English peas
3 c. cooked brown rice
1 (4 oz.) jar pimientos, diced
1 c. cooked lean ham, diced
6 green onions, chopped
4 hard-cooked egg whites,
　chopped
3/4 c. olives with pimientos,
　sliced

1/2 c. celery, chopped
2/3 c. sweet pickle relish
1 c. low-fat Cheddar
　cheese, shredded
1/3 c. plain nonfat yogurt
1/3 c. low-fat mayonnaise
12 lettuce leaves for
　garnish (optional)

1.　Cook peas according to package directions; drain and cool.
2.　Cook rice according to package directions.
3.　Combine peas and next 9 ingredients; stir well.
4.　Add yogurt and mayonnaise, tossing until mixed.
5.　Chill thoroughly; serve on lettuce leaves.

Yield: 12 servings
Per Serving:
　　185 cal, 6 gm fat, 10 gm pro, 24 gm carb, 12 mg chol, 604 mg sodium, 3 gm dietary fiber

Cold Pasta Salad

Nutrition Staff

6 to 8 cherry tomatoes
6 oz. pasta, cooked (3 c.)
1/2 c. feta cheese
1/3 c. low-calorie Italian
    dressing

1/4 c. green onions,
    chopped
2 T. pitted black olives,
    sliced
6 c. fresh spinach, washed
    & stems cut

1. Cut tomatoes in half and mix with remaining ingredients except spinach.
2. Arrange spinach on serving platter and arrange pasta mixture on top.

Yield: 4 servings
Per Serving:
    244 cal, 7 gm fat, 10 gm pro, 37 gm carb, 14 mg chol, 431 mg sodium, 4 gm dietary fiber

Confetti Cottage Cheese Salad

Cindy Kleckner, R.D.

1 (16 oz.) container low-
    fat cottage cheese
1/4 c. plain nonfat yogurt
1 c. carrots, shredded
3/4 c. tomato, chopped

3/4 c. green bell pepper,
    chopped
3 T. green onions, thinly
    sliced
1 tsp. oregano

1. In a medium bowl, combine all ingredients; mix well.
2. Serve chilled.

Yield: 5 servings
Per Serving (1 cup):
    95 cal, 1 gm fat, 13 gm pro, 8 gm carb, 10 mg chol, 398 mg sodium, 2 gm dietary fiber

Seasonal Fruit Salad

Georgia Kostas, M.P.H., R.D.

1 apple, chopped
1 banana, sliced
1 orange, sectioned

1 c. seasonal fruit of choice (seedless grapes, berries, melon, pine- apple, pear)

1. Combine fruit and serve immediately.

Yield: 8 servings
Per Serving (1/2 cup):
39 cal, 0 gm fat, 1 gm pro, 10 gm carb, 0 mg chol, 1 mg sodium, 1 gm dietary fiber

Apple Waldorf Salad

Nutrition Staff

1 Granny Smith apple
1 red delicious apple
1 T. lemon juice
1/2 c. celery, chopped
1 T. pecan halves, slightly chopped

1/4 c. plain nonfat yogurt
Dash of cinnamon
Dash of nutmeg
1 T. low-fat mayonnaise
Purple cabbage or lettuce leaves (optional)

1. Chop unpeeled apples; sprinkle with lemon juice.
2. Add all other ingredients; combine gently.
3. Serve on purple cabbage leaf or lettuce leaf.

Yield: 4 servings
Per Serving (1/2 cup):
76 cal, 3 gm fat, 1 gm pro, 13 gm carb, 1 mg chol, 37 mg sodium, 2 gm dietary fiber

*Substitute nonfat yogurt or blended
low-fat cottage cheese for sour cream.*

Cole Slaw

Veronica Coronado

1 med. head cabbage,
    chopped (16 oz.)
1 green pepper, chopped
3 carrots, peeled & grated
1/3 c. salad oil

3/4 c. white vinegar
1/2 c. honey
1/4 c. sugar
1 tsp. salt

1. Combine cabbage, green pepper and carrots in a large bowl.
2. Cook oil, white vinegar, honey, sugar and salt to near boil.
3. Pour over cabbage mixture and do not stir until cool, at least 30 minutes.
4. Refrigerate until ready to serve.

Yield: 16 servings
Per Serving:
    97 cal, 5 gm fat, 1 gm pro, 15 gm carb, 0 mg chol, 142 mg sodium, 1 gm dietary fiber

Sauté onions, green peppers and other vegetables in broth instead of fat.

Use a nonstick cooking spray -- it helps reduce fat and calories.

New Potato Salad with Mustard Vinaigrette

Veronica Coronado

4 lb. sm. red new potatoes,
  washed & unpeeled
4 green onions, chopped
1/2 c. fresh dill

1 recipe Mustard
  Vinaigrette
3/4 c. light sour cream

MUSTARD VINAIGRETTE DRESSING:

1/2 c. wine vinegar
2 T. Dijon-style mustard
1 tsp. salt

1/2 tsp. pepper
1/4 c. olive oil

1. Cook the potatoes in boiling water just until tender. Meanwhile, chop the green onion and dill. Reserve.
2. Drain the potatoes in a colander and run cold water over them.
3. Cut potatoes in quarters as soon as they can be handled and place in a large mixing bowl.
4. To prepare dressing, place all dressing ingredients except oil in a blender or food processor and process until all is combined (about 5 seconds). With the motor running, pour the oil in a slow, steady stream until incorporated.
5. Pour the dressing over the potatoes; add the reserved onion-dill mixture and toss gently.
6. Add the salt and pepper and fold in the sour cream. Let stand 30 minutes before serving.

Yield: 13 servings
Per Serving (1 cup):
  153 cal, 5 gm fat, 4 gm pro, 24 gm carb, 0 mg chol, 212 mg sodium, 2 gm dietary fiber

*Insoluble fiber in oats, fruits and vegetables
lowers cholesterol and regulates blood sugar.*

Potato Salad Italian Style

Jean Wisner, R.D.

2 lb. red new potatoes
Boiling water
1/2 c. green pepper, finely
    chopped
1/2 c. onion, finely chopped
1/2 c. celery, finely chopped
3 T. green olives, sliced
1/4 c. fat-free mayonnaise

1/4 c. nonfat plain yogurt
1 tsp. lemon juice
2 T. sweet pickle relish
1/2 tsp. basil, crushed
1/4 tsp. marjoram, crushed
1/4 tsp. rosemary, crushed
1/4 tsp. salt
1/4 tsp. pepper

1. Cook potatoes in boiling water until just tender when pierced, about 30 minutes. Drain. When cool, peel and cut into 1/2-inch cubes.
2. Combine the potatoes, green pepper, onion, celery and olives.
3. In a small bowl, stir together the mayonnaise, yogurt, lemon juice, pickle relish, basil, marjoram and rosemary. Pour over potatoes and mix well.
4. Season with salt and pepper.
5. Cover and chill at least 4 hours or overnight.

Yield: 8 servings
Per Serving:
    101 cal, 1 gm fat, 3 gm pro, 21 gm carb, 0 mg chol, 297 mg sodium, 3 gm dietary fiber

Southwestern Chicken Salad

Cindy Wachtler, R.D.

2 c. fresh spinach, torn
1/2 tomato
2 black olives
1/4 c. kidney beans
2 oz. boneless, skinless
    chicken breast
1 T. low-fat Cheddar
    cheese, grated

1/2 (6") corn tortillas, cut
    in strips & baked until
    crisp
2 T. picante sauce
1 T. corn relish
3 ears baby corn

1. Layer salad in order given.
2. Serve chilled.

Yield: 1 serving
Per Serving:
    308 cal, 6 gm fat, 30 gm pro, 37 gm carb, 52 mg chol, 460 mg sodium, 9 gm dietary fiber

Chicken-Wild Rice Salad

Walt Smith

1/2 c. wild rice, uncooked
2 c. poached chicken, diced
1 c. watercress leaves

1/2 c. green onion, thinly sliced
1/2 c. celery, diced
1/4 c. slivered almonds, toasted

TARRAGON VINAIGRETTE:
3 T. olive oil
3 T. white wine vinegar
1 T. fresh tarragon, chopped; or 1 tsp. dried, crumbled

1 tsp. salt
1/3 tsp. pepper
8 lettuce leaves

1. Cook rice according to package directions.
2. Rinse cooked rice under cold water and drain well. Transfer to a large bowl.
3. Add chicken, watercress, green onion, diced celery and almonds.
4. For vinaigrette, whisk oil gradually into vinegar.
5. Stir in tarragon, salt and pepper. Pour small amount of vinaigrette over chicken salad and toss gently, adding more vinaigrette a little at a time until evenly coated. Serve slightly chilled on lettuce leaves.

Yield: 8 servings
Per Serving:
182 cal, 9 gm fat, 15 gm pro, 10 gm carb, 33 mg chol, 307 mg sodium, 2 gm dietary fiber

If you take a vitamin-mineral supplement, choose
one that supplies no more than 100%
of the USRDA for the various nutrients.

Chicken Grape Salad
Veronica Coronado

4 (4 oz.) boneless, skin-
less chicken breasts
1 1/2 c. water
1 low-sodium bouillon cube
1 1/2 c. seedless green
grapes
1/4 c. pecan halves
1/3 c. diced celery
1/3 c. fresh dill, chopped

1/4 c. light sour cream
2 T. fat-free mayonnaise
2 T. low-fat mayonnaise
1/4 tsp. salt
1/4 tsp. pepper
2 bunches watercress
(optional)
Dill sprigs for garnish
(optional)

1. Preheat the oven to 350°F. Arrange the chicken breasts in a single layer in a shallow pan.
2. Bring the water to a boil and add the bouillon cube. Stir to dissolve. Pour enough bouillon in the baking pan to just cover the chicken breasts. Lay a sheet of aluminum foil over the chicken, and bake until cooked through, 30 minutes. Allow the chicken to cool in the liquid and discard liquid after cooling.
3. Shred the chicken into bite-size pieces and place in a large bowl. Add the grapes, pecans, celery and chopped dill. Toss well.
4. In a separate bowl, mix the sour cream and mayonnaise together. Toss this into the chicken salad. Season with salt and pepper. Cover and refrigerate for 2 hours.
5. Serve on a bed of watercress or other salad green garnished with dill sprigs.

Yield: 5 servings
Per Serving:
212 cal, 9 gm fat, 23 gm pro, 10 gm carb, 58 mg chol, 272 mg sodium, 1 gm dietary fiber

Air travel is dehydrating ... drink 1 cup of
water per hour of flight time.

Caribbean Chicken Salad Nutrition Staff

DRESSING:
1/2 c. plain nonfat yogurt

1/4 c. low-fat mayonnaise
1/4 tsp. cinnamon

SALAD:
16 oz. chicken breast strips
3/4 c. apple juice
3/4 c. water
1/2 c. long grain & wild rice, uncooked
3/4 c. McIntosh apple, un-peeled & chopped

1/2 c. celery, sliced
1/2 c. water chestnuts, chopped
30 seedless green grapes, cut into halves
Spinach leaves to garnish (optional)

1. Cook rice according to package directions.
2. Wash chicken pieces; pat dry. Set aside.
3. To prepare dressing, combine all ingredients in a small bowl; cover and refrigerate.
4. In a 2-quart saucepan, simmer chicken, apple juice and water, covered, over medium heat 15 to 20 minutes until juice runs clear when meat is pierced with fork. Remove chicken from pan and reserve juices for cooking rice.
5. Cut chicken in half-inch cubes; cover and chill.
6. Cook long grain and wild rice in cooking juices from chicken, adding water as needed, following label directions.
7. In a large bowl, gently toss together rice, apple, celery, water chestnuts and grapes; stir in chicken and dressing.
8. Serve on spinach leaves.

Yield: 6 servings
Per Serving (3/4 cup):
219 cal, 6 gm fat, 20 gm pro, 22 gm carb, 49 mg chol, 100 mg sodium, 1 gm dietary fiber

When purchasing frozen dinners, choose those which contain 10 grams of fat or less per 300 calorie meal.

Turkey Fruit Salad

Nutrition Staff

1/3 c. plain nonfat yogurt
1 T. low-fat mayonnaise
1 T. honey
1/2 tsp. orange peel, finely
   shredded
1/8 tsp. salt (optional)
1 c. cooked turkey (or
   chicken), cubed

1 c. fresh strawberries,
   halved
1 sm. banana, cut in 1/2"
   slices
1/2 c. celery, sliced
2 med. oranges, peeled &
   sections cut in half
4 lettuce leaves

1. Blend first 5 ingredients together; set aside.
2. Combine remaining ingredients in a separate bowl.
3. Fold the first mixture into the salad ingredients.
4. Chill.

Yield: 4 servings
Per Serving (1 cup):
   165 cal, 3 gm fat, 13 gm pro, 22 gm carb, 27 mg chol, 67 mg sodium,
   3 gm dietary fiber

Tuna Salad I

Nutrition Staff

1 (6 1/2 oz.) can water-
   packed tuna, drained
4 tsp. light Miracle Whip
4 T. plain nonfat yogurt
2 cooked egg whites,
   chopped

1/2 dill pickle, chopped
Onion powder, to taste
Pepper, to taste
1 or 2 T. apple, chopped
   (optional)

1. Combine all ingredients; mix well.

Yield: 2 servings
Per Serving (1/2 cup):
   180 cal, 4 gm fat, 30 gm pro, 5 gm carb, 16 mg chol, 890 mg sodium,
   0 gm dietary fiber

Tuna Salad II

Georgia Kostas, M.P.H., R.D.

1 (6 1/2 oz.) can water-
    packed tuna, drained
2 T. low-fat mayonnaise
1 T. lemon juice

1 celery stalk, diced
1 green onion, diced
2 T. apple, diced
3 sm. or 1 lg. sweet pickle

1.   Combine all ingredients.

Yield: 3 servings
Per Serving (1/2 cup):
    152 cal, 4 gm fat, 17 gm pro, 13 gm carb, 11 mg chol, 397 mg sodium,
    1 gm dietary fiber

Creamy Tuna Pasta Twist

Cindy Kleckner, R.D.

3 T. fat-free mayonnaise
3 T. low-fat mayonnaise
1/2 c. plain nonfat yogurt
2 T. cider vinegar
Dash of pepper
4 oz. twist macaroni, cooked
1 (6 1/2 oz.) can water-packed
    tuna, drained & flaked

1 c. cooked peas
1 c. celery, sliced
1/4 c. red onion, chopped
1 T. dill weed
1/4 c. green bell pepper,
    chopped

1.   In a large bowl, stir together first 4 ingredients until smooth.
2.   Add remaining ingredients; toss to coat well.
3.   Cover and chill.

Yield: 5 servings
Per Serving:
    211 cal, 4 gm fat, 15 gm pro, 28 gm carb, 15 mg chol, 345 mg sodium,
    3 gm dietary fiber

Salmon Salad

Cindy Kleckner, R.D.

1 (8 oz.) can red sockeye
  salmon, drained
1/2 c. orange juice
1/4 c. lemon juice
1 green bell pepper, chopped
1 sm. cucumber, chopped
1 sm. tomato, peeled, seeded
  & chopped

1/2 red onion, pared &
  minced
3 T. green onions, minced
4 lettuce leaves
4 lime wedges

1. In a large bowl, break salmon into bite-size pieces; crush bones.
2. Combine orange and lemon juice and pour over salmon; set aside.
3. Combine green pepper, cucumber, tomato and onions.
4. Add 1/3 of the vegetable mixture to the salmon mixture.
5. Marinate this combination and refrigerate for 2 to 3 hours.
6. To serve, arrange salmon salad on lettuce leaf; place reserved vegetables over salmon.
7. Serve with lime wedges.

Yield: 4 servings
Per Serving (1 cup):
    123 cal, 4 gm fat, 12 gm pro, 9 gm carb, 23 mg chol, 293 mg sodium, 2 gm dietary fiber

Tomato Aspic

Harriet Guthrie

1 sm. box lemon Jello,
  sugar-free
2 c. tomato juice
1/4 c. frozen green peas,
  thawed
1 T. cider vinegar
1/4 c. chives

1/4 c. green bell pepper,
  diced
1/2 c. celery, diced
Dash of pepper
4 lettuce leaves
Fresh parsley for garnish

1. Combine Jello and juice until thoroughly dissolved.
2. Add remaining ingredients.
3. Chill until set.
4. Serve on lettuce leaf.
5. Garnish with sprig of parsley.

Yield: 4 servings
Per Serving:
    45 cal, 0 gm fat, 3 gm pro, 8 gm carb, 0 mg chol, 515 mg sodium, 2 gm dietary fiber

Creamy Dill Salad Dressing

Chuck Coronado

1/2 c. low-fat cottage cheese	Freshly ground pepper, to taste
1/2 c. skim milk	1/2 c. low-fat mayonnaise
2 T. white wine vinegar	1 T. olive oil
1 clove garlic, crushed; or 1/2 tsp. minced garlic	1/8 tsp. sugar
	1 tsp. dill weed

1. Using a food processor, blend together all ingredients until smooth.

Yield: 27 servings
Per Serving (1 tablespoon):
24 cal, 2 gm fat, 1 gm pro, 1 gm carb, 1 mg chol, 34 mg sodium, 0 gm dietary fiber

Thousand Island Dressing

Cindy Wachtler, R.D.

1 c. plain nonfat yogurt	1 T. onion, minced
3 T. pickle relish	1 tsp. vinegar
3 T. chili sauce	1 tsp. mustard
2 T. low-fat mayonnaise	

1. Combine all ingredients in a small bowl; cover and refrigerate at least 1 hour.
2. Serve over salad greens.

Yield: 24 servings
Per Serving (1 tablespoon):
14 cal, <1 gm fat, 1 gm pro, 2 gm carb, 0 mg chol, 56 mg sodium, 0 gm dietary fiber

Bleu Cheese Yogurt Dressing

Jean Wisner, R.D.

1 c. plain nonfat yogurt
1/4 c. bleu cheese, crumbled

1/2 tsp. minced garlic
1/2 tsp. crushed tarragon

1. Combine all ingredients and blend well.
2. Store in container with a tight-fitting lid and store in refrigerator.

Yield: 20 servings
Per Serving (1 tablespoon):
  12 cal, <1 gm fat, 1 gm pro, 1 gm carb, 1 mg chol, 29 mg sodium, 0 gm dietary fiber

Ranch Dressing

Patty Kirk, R.D.

4 tsp. dry ranch or buttermilk salad dressing mix
1 c. skim milk

1/2 c. low-fat mayonnaise
1/2 c. plain nonfat yogurt

1. Blend with wire whisk milk, mayonnaise and yogurt.
2. Sprinkle dry dressing mix over above mixture and blend.
3. Chill.

Yield: 32 servings
Per Serving (1 tablespoon):
  18 cal, 1 gm fat, 1 gm pro, 1 gm carb, 1 mg chol, 87 mg sodium, 0 gm dietary fiber

One teaspoon of garlic salt contains 1,850 mg of sodium.
For garlic flavoring, use garlic powder instead.

Buttermilk Dressing

Nutrition Staff

1 c. low-fat buttermilk
1 c. low-fat cottage cheese
1 T. onion, chopped
1/4 tsp. minced garlic

2 T. lemon juice
1 tsp. sugar
1 tsp. chives

1. Blend all ingredients well in a container with a tight-fitting cover; shake well.
2. Chill.
3. Shake again before serving.

Yield: 20 servings
Per Serving (1 tablespoon):
14 cal, <1 gm fat, 2 gm pro, 1 gm carb, 1 mg chol, 59 sodium, 0 gm dietary fiber

Yogurt Dressing

Georgia Kostas, M.P.H., R.D.

2 tsp. lemon juice
1 T. oil
1/2 c. plain nonfat yogurt
1/2 tsp. mint

1/2 tsp. dill weed
1/8 tsp. garlic powder
   (optional)
1/8 tsp. onion powder (optional)

1. Mix all ingredients together in a blender on medium speed for 5 seconds. Keep refrigerated in covered jar.

Yield: 6 servings
Per Serving (1 tablespoon):
16 cal, 1 gm fat, 1 gm pro, 1 gm carb, 0 mg chol, 9 mg sodium, 0 gm dietary fiber

A 12-ounce can of diet cola contains 35-50 mg caffeine.

Lemon Mustard Dressing Nutrition Staff

1 T. olive oil
1 T. white wine
1 T. vinegar

1 T. fresh lemon juice
2 tsp. Dijon-style mustard
1/8 tsp. white pepper

1. In a small jar that has a tight-fitting cover, combine all ingredients; cover tightly and shake well.
2. Refrigerate until chilled.
3. Shake again before serving.

Yield: 4 servings
Per Serving (1 tablespoon):
36 cal, 3 gm fat, 0 gm pro, 1 gm carb, 0 mg chol, 33 mg sodium, 0 gm dietary fiber

Honey Mustard Dressing Nutrition Staff

1 T. olive oil
1 T. white wine
1 T. vinegar

1 T. honey
2 tsp. Dijon-style mustard
1/8 tsp. white pepper

1. In a small jar that has a tight-fitting cover, combine all ingredients; cover tightly and shake well.
2. Refrigerate until chilled.
3. Shake again before serving.

Yield: 4 servings
Per Serving (1 tablespoon):
51 cal, 3 gm fat, 0 gm pro, 4 gm carb, 0 mg chol, 33 mg sodium, 0 gm dietary fiber

Eat at least 20-35 grams of dietary fiber daily.

Orange Sesame Dressing

Jean Wisner, R.D.

1 c. plain nonfat yogurt
2 tsp. orange peel, grated
2 tsp. frozen orange juice
   concentrate

2 T. toasted sesame
   seeds

1. Blend all ingredients well.
2. Store in refrigerator in a container with a tight-fitting lid.

Yield: 19 servings
Per Servings (1 tablespoon):
   13 cal, 1 gm fat, 1 gm pro, 1 gm carb, 0 mg chol, 10 mg sodium, 0 gm
dietary fiber

Strawberry Vinaigrette Dressing

Veronica Coronado

1/4 c. Strawberry Vinegar
   (See Index)
1 1/2 tsp. vegetable oil

1/4 tsp. salt
1/4 tsp. pepper
1/4 tsp. sugar

1. Combine all ingredients.
2. Serve over your favorite salad.

Yield: 4 servings
Per Serving (1 tablespoon):
   20 cal, 2 gm fat, 0 gm pro, 2 gm carb, 0 mg chol, 133 mg sodium, 0 gm
dietary fiber

There is no "magic" food or supplement available
on the market that provides good health.

Tomato Vinaigrette Dressing

Jean Wisner, R.D.

1/2 c. tomato juice
1/4 c. apple cider vinegar
1/4 c. lemon juice
1/4 c. vegetable oil
1 tsp. thyme

1 tsp. minced garlic
1 tsp. pepper
5 green onions, chopped
2/3 c. fresh parsley,
   chopped

1. Place all ingredients in food processor or blender.
2. Blend on high speed for 10 to 15 seconds.

Yield: 32 servings
Per Serving (1 tablespoon):
18 cal, 2 gm fat, 0 gm pro, 1 gm carb, 0 mg chol, 13 mg sodium, 0 gm dietary fiber

Pineapple-Sesame Dressing

Jean Wisner, R.D.

1/2 c. pineapple juice
1/3 c. vinegar
1/3 c. green onions, finely
   chopped
1/3 c. fresh parsley, finely
   chopped
1 T. Dijon-style mustard

Dash of light soy sauce
2 T. vinegar
1 T. olive oil
2 T. sesame seeds
1/4 tsp. minced garlic
1/4 tsp. ginger powder
1/4 tsp. paprika

1. Blend all ingredients thoroughly with a fork.
2. Pour over fresh salad greens.

Yield: 30 servings
Per Serving (1 tablespoon):
11 cal, 1 gm fat, 0 gm pro, 1 gm carb, 0 mg chol, 7 mg sodium, 0 gm dietary fiber

Fresh Basil Dressing

Jeanne Rumley

2 T. fresh basil, minced
1/3 c. red wine vinegar
1 1/2 T. lemon juice
1 T. olive oil

1 T. water
1 tsp. minced garlic
1/4 tsp. pepper

1. Combine all ingredients, cover, and chill for 1 hour before using.
2. Store in refrigerator in a container with a tight-fitting lid.

Yield: 8 servings
Per Serving (1 tablespoon):
    18 cal, 2 gm fat, 0 gm pro, 1 gm carb, 0 mg chol, 0 mg sodium, 0 gm
    dietary fiber

Nick's Zero
Salad Dressing

Nick Koustis

3 c. V-8 vegetable juice
3/4 c. lemon juice
1 1/2 T. onion, chopped

4 tsp. fresh parsley,
    chopped; or 2 tsp.
    dried parsley

1. Combine all ingredients in a blender; blend.

Yield: 62 servings.
Per Serving (1 tablespoon):
    3 cal, 0 gm fat, 0 gm pro, 1 gm carb, 0 mg chol, 38 mg sodium, 0 gm
    dietary fiber

Fresh
from the
Garden

Fresh from the Garden

Fresh from the Garden

Sweet and Dilly Carrots

Veronica Coronado

2 c. carrots, peeled & sliced
1 T. margarine
2 T. honey

1/4 tsp. lemon pepper
1/8 tsp. salt
1/8 tsp. dill weed

1. Place 1/4 cup water in a glass dish.
2. Add the carrots; cover dish and microwave for 5 minutes or until carrots are tender.
3. Drain the cooked carrots well and put them in a serving dish.
4. Add all the remaining ingredients; mix well.
5. Serve hot.

Yield: 4 servings
Per Serving (1/2 cup):
94 cal, 3 gm fat, 1 gm pro, 17 gm carb, 0 mg chol, 152 mg sodium, 2 gm dietary fiber

Party Carrots

Harriet Guthrie

3 3/4 c. carrots, sliced
5 T. honey
1/2 c. apples, diced
1/2 c. raisins
1 T. lemon juice

1 T. margarine
1 T. flour
1 (8 oz.) can unsweetened crushed pineapple, drained

1. Steam carrots until firm-soft; drain.
2. Stir in honey, lemon juice and margarine.
3. Stir in flour, raisins, pineapple and apple.
4. Heat until bubbly; serve.

Yield: 11 servings
Per Serving (1/2 cup):
95 cal, 1 gm fat, 1 gm pro, 22 gm carb, 0 mg chol, 49 mg sodium, 2 gm dietary fiber

Italian Green Beans
Veronica Coronado

1 lb. fresh green beans	1/2 c. dry white wine
2 1/2 tsp. olive oil	1/2 c. pitted black olives
1 lg. onion, coarsely	1 T. lemon juice
chopped	1/2 tsp. freshly ground
2 tsp. minced garlic	pepper
4 lg. tomatoes, peeled,	
seeded & coarsely	
chopped	

1. Steam green beans until crisp-tender.
2. Drain, rinse under cold water and drain again; set the beans aside.
3. Heat the oil in a large skillet over medium heat; add onion and garlic.
4. Cook for 5 minutes.
5. Add the tomatoes and wine; cook for 20 minutes.
6. Toss in the olives and reserved beans; heat through, 3 minutes.
7. Sprinkle with lemon juice and pepper; serve immediately.

Yield: 6 servings
Per Serving (1/2 cup):
105 cal, 4 gm fat, 3 gm pro, 14 gm carb, 0 mg chol, 130 mg sodium, 4 gm dietary fiber

Sesame Broccoli
Nutrition Staff

1 T. sesame seeds,	2 tsp. olive oil or
toasted	safflower oil
3 c. fresh broccoli, trimmed	1 T. vinegar
& cut into spears	1 T. light soy sauce

1. Toast sesame seeds on a cookie sheet in oven on low heat; remove.
2. Steam broccoli until tender-crisp.
3. In a saucepan, combine oil, vinegar, soy sauce and toasted sesame seeds.
4. Heat until boiling.
5. Pour sauce over broccoli, turning to coat evenly.

Yield: 4 servings
Per Serving:
67 cal, 4 gm fat, 5 gm pro, 7 gm carb, 0 mg chol, 163 mg sodium, 3 gm dietary fiber

Lemon Spinach Sauté

Victoria Williams

2 lb. fresh spinach
1 1/2 T. olive oil

2 T. fresh lemon juice
1/4 c. pine nuts or sliced almonds

1. Wash spinach and drain, leaving a small amount of water on leaves.
2. Place spinach in large pot and sauté for 3 to 4 minutes until slightly wilted.
3. Drain spinach in colander.
4. Add olive oil and pine nuts or almonds to pot and sauté until lightly browned.
5. Return spinach to pot and mix with olive oil and pine nuts.
6. Add lemon juice, warm through and serve immediately.

Yield: 8 servings
Per Serving:
   72 cal, 5 gm fat, 4 gm pro, 5 gm carb, 0 mg chol, 92 mg sodium, 3 gm dietary fiber

Spinach Casserole

Georgia Kostas, M.P.H., R. D.

2 (10 oz.) pkg. frozen chopped spinach, thawed
1 c. low-fat cottage cheese
1/2 pkg. dry onion soup mix

2 tsp. dill weed
1/4 c. part-skim mozzarella
   cheese, grated
1/2 c. water chestnuts,
   sliced (optional)

1. Cook spinach according to package directions; drain and squeeze out excess water.
2. In a blender container, combine cottage cheese, soup mix and dill weed; blend.
3. Preheat oven to 350°F.
4. Combine mozzarella cheese and water chestnuts with cottage cheese mixture; mix well.
5. Pour into covered casserole dish or Pyrex dish; bake for 1 hour.

Yield: 6 servings
Per Serving:
   64 cal, 2 gm fat, 9 gm pro, 5 gm carb, 7 mg chol, 298 mg sodium, 2 gm dietary fiber

Savory Spinach Rice Casserole

Georgia Kostas, M.P.H., R.D.

1 med. onion, chopped
2 tsp. olive oil
3 lb. spinach, well washed
   & torn into lg. pieces;
   or 3 (10 oz.) pkg. frozen
   spinach, thawed &
   squeezed of excess
   water
1 T. tomato purée (catsup)

2 tsp. minced garlic
2 or 3 scallions; or 1/2 c.
   green onions, diced
3 T. fresh parsley
1/8 tsp. salt
2 T. fresh dill weed
1/8 tsp. pepper
1 c. brown rice, uncooked

1. In a wide saucepan, sauté onion, garlic and scallions in oil until onion is golden brown.
2. Add the spinach; continue stirring until all the spinach is lightly cooked.
3. Add the tomato purée, parsley, dill, salt and pepper.
4. Simmer for 15 to 30 minutes, stirring occasionally.
5. In the meantime, cook the rice in a separate saucepan.
6. Mix rice with the spinach; add a little more water, if necessary, and allow to simmer until all the water has evaporated.

Yield: 8 servings
Per Serving:
   147 cal, 2 gm fat, 7 gm pro, 27 gm carb, 0 mg chol, 189 mg sodium, 6 gm dietary fiber

To maximize nutrient value, cook vegetables in
a minimum amount of water or steam them.

Easy Squash Casserole

Veronica Coronado

1 lb. yellow summer squash	1 tsp. margarine
1/4 c. water	2 tsp. sugar
1/3 c. onion, chopped	1/4 tsp. salt
1/4 c. bread crumbs	1/4 tsp. pepper

1. Rinse and slice squash; place in a glass dish.
2. Add water and onion; cover and microwave until squash is tender.
3. Drain squash and onion well.
4. Put squash and onion in bowl; add remaining ingredients and mix well.
5. Preheat oven to 350°F.
6. Place mixture in a baking dish and bake until hot, 20 to 30 minutes.

Yield: 4 servings
Per Serving:
> 65 cal, 2 gm fat, 2 gm pro, 13 gm carb, 0 mg chol, 186 mg sodium, 2 gm dietary fiber

Add grated carrots, onions, mushrooms
and green peppers to spaghetti, meat
or pizza sauce to increase vegetables in your diet.

Fall Spaghetti Squash with Vegetables

Cindy Wachtler, R.D.

1 spaghetti squash
   (approx. 2 1/2 to 3 lb.)
2 c. tomatoes, chopped
2 1/2 tsp. olive oil
1/2 tsp. minced garlic
4 lg. fresh basil leaves,
   chopped
1/8 tsp. pepper

1 1/2 c. broccoli florets,
   stems sliced thin &
   florets halved
1 lg. carrot, sliced thin
   diagonally
2 T. water
2 oz. snow peas, trimmed &
   sliced thin diagonally
2 T. Parmesan cheese

1. Pierce squash through to the center with thin, sharp knife 6 times; microwave on high 6 minutes; turn squash over and microwave 6 minutes more.
2. Remove from microwave; cover with kitchen towel or inverted bowl and let stand 10 minutes.
3. Combine tomatoes, oil and garlic in a 2-or 3-quart round microwave-safe casserole; microwave uncovered 3 minutes or until tomatoes are softened, stirring once.
4. Add basil and pepper to taste; set aside.
5. Place broccoli and carrots in 10-inch microwave-safe glass pie plate; add the 2 tablespoons water. Cover loosely with wax paper. Microwave 2 minutes; stir in snow peas.
6. Microwave covered 1 minute more, or until vegetables are tender; let stand covered 5 minutes.
7. Meanwhile, halve squash lengthwise; discard seeds and center pith.
8. With fork, pull squash from shell and add directly to tomato sauce in casserole.
9. Drain vegetables and add to casserole; fluff with fork.
10. Sprinkle with cheese and serve immediately.

Yield: 4 servings
Per Serving:
   119 cal, 4 gm fat, 6 gm pro, 18 gm carb, 2 mg chol, 80 mg sodium, 6 gm dietary fiber

*Most fruits and vegetables contain 1
to 3 grams of fiber per 1/2 cup.*

Autumn Stuffed Acorn Squash

Kim Ross

2 sm. acorn squash, seeded & halved	1/2 c. zucchini, thickly sliced
2 tsp. olive oil	1/2 c. mushrooms, thickly sliced
1/2 c. onion, diced	
1/2 c. carrots, diced	1/2 tsp. minced garlic
1/2 c. red bell pepper, diced	Nonstick vegetable cooking spray

1. Preheat oven to 350°F.
2. Spray a large baking dish with cooking spray.
3. Steam acorn squash halves in microwave, placing cut sides down in pan with 1/4 cup water for 10 to 15 minutes.
4. Spray medium skillet with cooking spray; add olive oil and heat.
5. Sauté remaining ingredients 5 minutes only, stirring frequently.
6. Spoon vegetables into squash halves; bake 20 to 25 minutes or until squash is tender.

Yield: 4 servings
Per Serving (1/2 squash):
  84 cal, 3 gm fat, 2 gm pro, 15 gm carb, 0 mg chol, 16 mg sodium, 4 gm dietary fiber

Stuffed Acorn Squash

Nutrition Staff

2 acorn squash, cut in half	1 c. green peas (if fresh, cooked & if frozen, thawed)
1 tsp. apple juice	
2 to 3 tsp. brown sugar	
1/2 tsp. cinnamon	4 tsp. diet margarine

1. Place squash halves cut-side-down in shallow baking pan; cover bottom with water.
2. Bake at 400°F. for 50 to 60 minutes or until tender.
3. Turn squash over.
4. Mix apple juice, brown sugar and cinnamon together; coat each squash cavity with mixture.
5. Fill each squash cavity with 1/4 cup peas and dot each with 1 teaspoon margarine.
6. Continue baking until apple juice mixture is bubbly, about 15 minutes.

Yield: 4 servings
Per Serving (1/2 squash):
  118 cal, 3 gm fat, 3 gm pro, 22 gm carb, 0 mg chol, 86 mg sodium, 7 gm dietary fiber

Orange Beets

Harriet Guthrie

1 lb. can sliced beets,
 drained
1/2 c. orange juice
1 T. honey
1 T. margarine

1 T. cornstarch
1 tsp. water
1 1/2 tsp. orange rind,
 grated

1. In a 1 1/2-quart saucepan, heat orange juice, honey and margarine.
2. Combine cornstarch with water and add to juice mixture; stir until mixture thickens.
3. Add beets and orange rind; heat thoroughly.

Yield: 5 servings
Per Serving (1/2 cup):
 84 cal, 2 gm fat, 1 gm pro, 14 gm carb, 0 mg chol, 373 mg sodium, 2 gm dietary fiber

Eggplant Caponata

Nutrition Staff

1 lg. eggplant (whole)
4 green onions, chopped
1 lg. tomato, chopped
2 T. parsley
1/2 tsp. minced garlic

3 T. white wine vinegar or
 tarragon vinegar
2 1/2 tsp. vegetable oil
1/4 tsp. salt
1/2 tsp. oregano
Freshly ground pepper

1. Slice whole eggplant into fourths; place in shallow pan and add water to fill 1/4-inch deep.
2. Bake at 375°F. for 30 minutes.
3. Remove from oven, drain and rinse in cool water.
4. Pat dry and peel off skin; dice small.
5. Mix all ingredients lightly with eggplant.
6. Chill several hours to blend.

Yield: 4 servings
Per Serving (3/4 cup):
 69 cal, 3 gm fat, 2 gm pro, 11 gm carb, 0 mg chol, 147 mg sodium, 3 gm dietary fiber

Baked Eggplant Stuffing

Jean Wisner, R.D.

6 c. eggplant, peeled &
   cubed
1/2 c. green onions,
   chopped
1/4 c. green bell pepper,
   chopped
1/4 c. red bell pepper,
   chopped

2 c. bread crumbs
1/2 c. evaporated skimmed
   milk
2 egg whites
3/4 tsp. seasoning salt
3/4 c. low-fat Cheddar
   cheese

1. Place eggplant, onion and peppers in a 13x9x2-inch microwave dish; microwave on high 15 to 20 minutes.
2. Drain well.
3. Combine remaining ingredients except cheese and spoon over vegetables.
4. Top with cheese and bake in oven at 375°F. for 25 minutes.

Yield: 12 servings
Per Serving:
   104 cal, 2 gm fat, 6 gm pro, 16 gm carb, 4 mg chol, 249 mg sodium, 2 gm dietary fiber

One cup of broccoli is an excellent source of vitamins A and C, contains 3 grams of fiber, and is only about 45 calories.

Harvest Corn Casserole
Harriet Guthrie

1/2 green bell pepper,
   chopped
1/2 onion, finely chopped
2 T. margarine
2 T. flour
1/2 tsp. salt
1/4 tsp. paprika
1/2 tsp. dry mustard

1 c. skim milk
1/2 c. bread cubes, dry
1 tsp. margarine
2 c. whole corn, frozen
1/4 c. egg substitute
1/2 c. bread crumbs
Nonstick vegetable
   cooking spray

1. Cook pepper and onion in 2 tablespoons margarine for 5 minutes, stirring constantly.
2. Add flour mixed with seasonings; stir until blended.
3. Add skim milk and cook until thick.
4. Brown bread cubes in 1 teaspoon margarine and add with corn and egg substitute.
5. Turn into baking dish sprayed with cooking spray; cover with crumbs.
6. Bake at 350°F. for 45 minutes to 1 hour until set.

Yield: 8 servings
Per Serving:
   121 cal, 4 gm fat, 4 gm pro, 18 gm carb, 1 mg chol, 257 mg sodium, 2 gm dietary fiber

Corn and Rice Casserole
Brenda Mack

2 c. cooked brown rice
4 oz. low-fat Cheddar
   cheese
1 c. frozen corn
1 c. celery, chopped
1 sm. onion, chopped

1 c. skim milk
Pepper, to taste
3 T. almonds, slivered
Nonstick vegetable
   cooking spray

1. Spray skillet with cooking spray and brown celery and onion.
2. Cut cheese into 1/2-inch cubes; mix together with rice, corn, celery, onion, skim milk, pepper and almonds.
3. Bake at 350°F. for 30 minutes.

Yield: 12 servings
Per Serving (1/2 cup):
   105 cal, 3 gm fat, 5 gm pro, 14 gm carb, 5 mg chol, 71 mg sodium, 2 gm dietary fiber

Garden Brown Rice Pilaf

Cindy Wachtler, R.D.

1 tsp. margarine
2 med. carrots, peeled & chopped
1/2 c. green onions, chopped
2 garlic cloves, minced
1 c. brown rice, uncooked
2 c. water
1/4 c. sherry
1/4 c. fresh parsley, chopped

1 tsp. chicken-flavored bouillon granules
1/4 tsp. pepper
1 c. fresh mushrooms, sliced
2 T. Parmesan cheese
Nonstick vegetable cooking spray

1. Coat large skillet with cooking spray; add margarine.
2. Place over medium heat until margarine melts; add carrots, green onions and garlic. Sauté until tender.
3. Add rice; cook over low heat 1 minute, stirring constantly.
4. Add water and next 4 ingredients; bring to a boil
5. Cover, reduce heat and simmer 45 minutes or until liquid is absorbed.
6. Coat small skillet with cooking spray; place over medium heat until hot.
7. Add mushrooms and sauté until tender.
8. Add to rice mixture; stir to heat.
9. Remove from heat and sprinkle with Parmesan cheese.

Yield: 8 servings
Per serving:
117 cal, 1 gm fat, 3 gm pro, 21 gm carb, 1 mg chol, 163 mg sodium, 2 gm dietary fiber

The peel and skins of carrots and potatoes are high in fiber and nutrients.

Twice Baked Potatoes

Veronica Coronado

10 lg. potatoes
1 c. light sour cream
1 c. low-fat cottage cheese
1 tsp. salt
1/2 tsp. pepper

2 T. onion flakes
1 T. parsley
1/4 c. skim milk
5 oz. low-fat Cheddar
   cheese, shredded

1. Bake potatoes at 375°F. for 1 1/2 hours until soft.
2. Slice potatoes in half lengthwise. Scoop out potato, saving the skin.
3. Mash potatoes. Add remaining ingredients except Cheddar cheese; blend together until smooth.
4. Fill potato skins and top with 1 tablespoon Cheddar cheese.
5. Bake at 350°F. for 20 minutes or until hot.
6. Can be made ahead of time and refrigerated up to 3 days or frozen.

Yield: 20 servings
Per Serving (1/2 potato):
   185 cal, 2 gm fat, 7 gm pro, 35 gm carb, 5 mg chol, 215 mg sodium, 6 gm dietary fiber

Garlic Roasted Potatoes

Cindy Wachtler, R.D.

6 med. baking potatoes
2 T. olive oil
1 T. minced garlic; or
   1/4 tsp. garlic powder

1/2 tsp. salt
1/2 tsp. freshly ground
   pepper

1. Preheat oven to 450°F. Place a nonstick baking sheet in the oven to preheat (or spray a regular baking sheet with nonstick vegetable cooking spray).
2. Peel the potatoes and cut each lengthwise down the center and then into 2-inch cubes.
3. Toss the potato cubes with the remaining ingredients.
4. Lay the potato cubes on the baking sheet and bake for 30 minutes, turning them with a strong spatula a few times so that all sides brown.

Yield: 6 servings
Per Serving (1 potato):
   134 cal, 5 gm fat, 3 gm pro, 21 gm carb, 0 mg chol, 182 mg sodium, 2 gm dietary fiber

Herb Roasted Potatoes

Nutrition Staff

3 or 4 med. baking potatoes,
thinly sliced (approx. 1 lb.)
1/4 c. chives, minced
2 T. parsley

1/4 tsp. pepper
1/2 tsp. paprika
1 tsp. rosemary
Nonstick vegetable cooking spray

1. Mix chives, parsley, pepper, paprika and rosemary together in a small bowl.
2. Layer 1/3 of potatoes in an 8x8x2-inch baking pan sprayed with cooking spray.
3. Sprinkle with 1/3 herb mixture.
4. Repeat layers until all ingredients are used; cover with foil.
5. Bake at 350°F. for 45 minutes or until done.

Yield: 5 servings
Per Serving:
107 cal, 0 gm fat, 3 gm pro, 25 gm carb, 0 mg chol, 13 mg sodium, 4 gm dietary fiber

Caraway Potatoes

Veronica Coronado

2 lg. baking potatoes,
quartered
1 sm. onion, finely-
chopped
1 T. margarine
1 T. Parmesan cheese

1 tsp. caraway seed,
crushed a bit
1/2 tsp. nutmeg (optional)
1/4 c. skim milk
1/4 tsp. salt
1/4 tsp. pepper

1. In a medium saucepan, bring potatoes to a boil in enough water to cover.
2. Cover, lower temperature and boil potatoes until tender, about 15 to 20 minutes; drain.
3. In a medium sauté pan, sauté onion in margarine until tender.
4. Add to potatoes, along with Parmesan cheese, caraway seed and nutmeg.
5. Mash potatoes, adding milk as needed to keep mixture moist but still fairly stiff.
6. Season with salt and pepper, and serve.

Yield: 4 servings
Per Serving:
189 cal, 4 gm fat, 5 gm pro, 36 gm carb, 1 mg chol, 208 mg sodium, 6 gm dietary fiber

Sweet Potato Pie Casserole

Nutrition Staff

1 1/2 lb. peeled sweet pota-
    toes or yams, thinly
    sliced
1/4 tsp. salt (optional)
1/8 tsp. white pepper
1 T. plus 1 tsp. margarine,
    melted

1/4 tsp. ground cinnamon
2 T. orange juice
    concentrate, undiluted
1 c. miniature
    marshmallows
Nonstick vegetable
    cooking spray

1. Preheat oven to 350°F.
2. Soak potato slices in cold water to cover for 5 minutes; drain; using paper towels, pat dry.
3. Spray an 8 or 9-inch pie plate with cooking spray.
4. Arrange potato slices in plate in an overlapping concentric circular pattern; sprinkle with salt and pepper.
5. Cover with foil and bake until slices are just tender, about 45 minutes.
6. Remove plate from oven and turn oven to broil.
7. Combine melted margarine, cinnamon and orange juice; drizzle over pie.
8. Bake until edges begin to brown, about 10 minutes.
9. Remove from oven and top with marshmallows.
10. Broil for 3 minutes, or until marshmallows are lightly browned.

Yield: 8 servings
Per Serving (1 piece):
    135 cal, 2 gm fat, 2 gm pro, 28 carb, 0 mg chol, 38 mg sodium, 2 gm dietary fiber

*Calorie-free club soda adds pizzaz to iced fruit juices,
makes them go farther, and reduces calories per portion.*

Mushroom Apple Stuffing

Jean Wisner, R.D.

1/2 c. onion, minced
2 tsp. chicken bouillon
　　granules
8 oz. fresh mushrooms
2 T. Butter Buds
1 c. water
4 med. green apples, chopped
1 tsp. cinnamon

1 tsp. nutmeg
1 tsp. sage
1 tsp. pepper
1 tsp. curry
1/4 c. parsley
4 slices bread, toasted &
　　cubed
1 c. water

1. Brown first 5 ingredients in a nonstick skillet.
2. Add next 9 ingredients and simmer until apples are tender.
3. Place dressing in an 8-inch square casserole dish.
4. Cover and bake at 350°F. for 30 to 40 minutes.

Yield: 4 servings
Per Serving:
　　196 cal, 2 gm fat, 5 gm pro, 41 gm carb, 0 mg chol, 649 mg sodium,
　　5 gm dietary fiber

Beans Supreme

Harriet Guthrie

1 (15 oz.) can pinto beans
1 (15 oz.) can black-eyed
　　peas
1 (15 oz.) can lima beans
1 (15 oz.) can kidney beans
2 (15 oz.) cans pork & beans
2 lb. lean ground round
1 lg. onion, chopped

1 green bell pepper,
　　chopped
2 c. ketchup
1 c. burgundy wine
1/2 c. brown sugar
1 T. worcestershire sauce
1 T. dry mustard

1. Rinse and drain all beans except pork and beans.
2. Brown beef with onion and green pepper; drain fat.
3. Add to beans.
4. Stir in remaining ingredients.
5. Bake at 350°F. for 1 hour.

Yield: 20 servings
Per Serving (1 cup):
　　270 cal, 7 gm fat, 16 gm pro, 34 gm carb, 29 mg chol, 612 mg sodium,
　　7 gm dietary fiber

Notes and Recipes

_____

_____

_____

_____

_____

_____

_____

_____

_____

_____

_____

_____

Poultry
with
Pizzaz

Poultry with Pizzaz

Poultry with Pizzaz

Southern Fried Chicken   Patty Kirk, R.D.

6 (4 oz.) boneless, skinless
   chicken breasts
1 T. vegetable oil
1/3 c. flour
1/2 tsp. seasoned salt

1/2 tsp. paprika
1/4 tsp. garlic powder
1/8 tsp. pepper
Nonstick vegetable
   cooking spray

1. Wash chicken pieces; leave slightly moist.
2. Select a large nonstick skillet; spray with cooking spray.
3. Combine flour and spices in a plastic bag or bowl; shake or roll chicken, one or two pieces at a time, in seasoned flour. Set aside on wax paper.
4. Heat oil in the skillet, then add chicken.
5. Brown over medium heat for about 10 to 12 minutes on each side, until golden brown on all sides.

Yield: 6 servings
Per Serving:
   185 cal, 5 gm fat, 27 gm pro, 5 gm carb, 72 mg chol, 169 mg sodium, 0 mg dietary fiber

Remove the skin and fat from a 3-pound chicken
and you save approximately 1745 calories.

Chicken Cacciatore

Cindy Kleckner, R.D.

2 1/2 to 3 lb. boneless,
skinless chicken breasts
1 to 1 1/2 T. margarine
1/4 c. flour
2 c. onion rings, thinly
sliced
1/2 c. green bell pepper,
chopped

1 tsp. minced garlic
1 (16 oz.) can tomatoes,
low-sodium
1 (4 oz.) can tomato
sauce, low-sodium
1/2 c. fresh mushrooms,
sliced
1/4 tsp. oregano

1. Wash chicken and pat dry.
2. Melt margarine in electric skillet.
3. Coat chicken with flour.
4. Cook chicken over medium heat until light brown, about 15 to 20 minutes.
5. Remove chicken; set aside.
6. Add onion rings, green pepper and garlic to skillet; cook and stir over medium heat until onion and green pepper are tender.
7. Stir in remaining ingredients.
8. Add chicken to sauce; cover tightly and simmer for 30 to 40 minutes, until thickest pieces are fork-tender.
9. Serve with rice, noodles or spaghetti.

Yield: 6 servings
Per Serving:
342 cal, 8 gm fat, 51 gm pro, 14 gm carb, 132 chol, 159 mg sodium, 3 gm dietary fiber

Exercise has the beneficial impact of raising
HDL (good) cholesterol levels.

Chicken Broccoli Casserole

Nutrition Staff

6 (4 oz.) boneless, skinless
   chicken breasts
2 (10 oz.) pkg. frozen
   broccoli spears
1 T. margarine
2 T. flour

2 c. skim milk
1/2 tsp. chicken bouillon
   granules
1/4 tsp. pepper
1/4 tsp. nutmeg
1/2 c. Parmesan cheese

1. Wash chicken pieces; pat dry. Set aside.
2. Thaw and drain broccoli according to package directions.
3. Arrange chicken and broccoli in a 13x9x2-inch casserole dish. Chicken may be cut into strips if desired.
4. Make a thin cream sauce by melting margarine in saucepan; add flour.
5. Gradually add the milk and cook until sauce thickens.
6. Add bouillon granules, nutmeg, pepper and half of the Parmesan cheese.
7. Pour mixture over chicken and broccoli; sprinkle remaining Parmesan cheese over sauce.
8. Bake, uncovered, in a preheated 350° oven for about 30 to 35 minutes or until bubbly.

Yield: 6 servings
Per Servings:
   254 cal, 7 gm fat, 35 gm pro, 11 gm carb, 79 mg chol, 357 mg sodium, 2 gm dietary fiber

*You burn 7 to 10 calories per minute
during aerobic exercise.*

Chicken Breasts in Orange Sauce

Veronica Coronado

6 (4 oz.) chicken breasts	1/2 tsp. salt
1 1/2 T. margarine	2 T. water
2 T. flour	1 c. orange juice
2 T. sugar	1/2 c. water
1/4 tsp. dry mustard	3 c. cooked brown rice
1/4 tsp. cinnamon	1 orange, sliced (optional)
1/8 tsp. ginger	Parsley (optional)

1. Brown chicken breasts in margarine in skillet; remove.
2. Add flour, sugar, spices and salt to drippings in skillet; stir in 2 tablespoons water.
3. Stir to make a smooth paste.
4. Gradually stir in orange juice and 1/2 cup water; cook, stirring constantly until mixture thickens and comes to a boil
5. Add chicken breasts; cover and simmer over low heat until tender, about 20 minutes.
6. Remove chicken to serving platter.
7. Serve with hot rice and sauce.
8. Garnish with orange slices and parsley, if desired.

Yield: 6 servings
Per Serving:
330 cal, 7 gm fat, 30 gm pro, 37 gm carb, 72 mg chol, 275 mg sodium, 2 gm dietary fiber

Toss rice with a fork--a spoon bruises
the grains and makes them sticky.

Chicken Piccata

Chuck Coronado

1 sm. onion, peeled &
   chopped
1 tsp. minced garlic
5 green onions, chopped
1 tsp. olive oil
8 (4 oz.) boneless, skin-
   less chicken breasts
1/2 c. flour
1/2 tsp. salt
1/2 tsp. pepper

2 T. margarine
2 T. sherry
2 T. lemon juice
1 T. capers, chopped
2 T. chicken broth
8 lemon slices, thinly
   sliced (optional)
2 T. parsley
16 oz. angel hair pasta, cooked
Nonstick vegetable cooking spray

1. Spray skillet with nonstick spray. Sauté the onion, garlic and green onions in the olive oil just until tender; remove from the pan and set aside.
2. Pound chicken breasts flat with a meat pounder.
3. Mix the flour, salt and pepper together, and place in a flat bowl.
4. Dip the chicken slices into the flour mixture.
5. Lightly brown chicken slices in margarine, 2 to 3 minutes per side; add the sautéed onions and garlic.
6. Over high heat, add the sherry, lemon juice, capers and chicken broth.
7. Serve over pasta and garnish with thin slices of lemon and parsley.

Yield: 8 servings
Per Serving:
   403 cal, 8 gm fat, 34 gm pro, 46 gm carb, 72 mg chol, 186 mg sodium, 2 gm dietary fiber

A 5-ounce cup of coffee contains 100 mg of caffeine--
limit your intake to 2 cups daily.

Indian Baked Chicken

John Baer

4 (4 oz.) skinless chicken breasts

MARINADE:

1 tsp. ground cumin
1 tsp. paprika
1 tsp. turmeric
1 to 1 1/2 tsp. cayenne
    pepper

1 tsp. freshly ground
    pepper
2 - 3 cloves garlic, minced
8 T. lemon juice

1. Clean chicken breasts and pat dry; set aside.
2. Combine marinade ingredients and mix well.
3. Place chicken in a baking dish and add marinade; cover with plastic wrap.
4. Marinate 24 hours in refrigerator.
5. When ready to bake, preheat oven to 400°F.
6. Remove chicken from marinade. Reserve marinade.
7. Bake 20 minutes on 1 side. Turn chicken and bake an additional 25 minutes, basting occasionally with marinade while cooking.

Yield: 4 servings
Per Serving:
    155 cal, 3 gm fat, 27 gm pro, 3 gm carb, 72 mg chol, 64 mg sodium, 0 gm dietary fiber

    *Nutrient analysis includes 75% of the marinade ingredients.

For better barbecues, microwave chicken pieces until partially done, then finish on grill. They'll be moist and have charcoal flavor.

Parmesan Chicken with Asparagus

Veronica Coronado

8 (4 oz.) boneless, skinless
   chicken breasts
2 c. plain nonfat yogurt
1 1/2 (10 3/4 oz) cans cream
   of asparagus soup
5 oz. canned mushrooms,
   drained

1/2 c. white wine
3/4 c. Parmesan cheese,
   divided
1 1/2 lb. fresh asparagus,
   partially cooked
Nonstick vegetable
   cooking spray

1. Remove tough end of asparagus by breaking off end.
2. Spray a large skillet with cooking spray. Brown chicken breasts. Remove and place chicken in a 13x9x2-inch baking dish.
3. Combine the yogurt, soup, mushrooms and white wine.
4. Pour 1/4 of this sauce over chicken; sprinkle 1/2 cup Parmesan cheese over sauce.
5. Layer the asparagus over cheese and add remaining sauce.
6. Top with remaining cheese and bake at 350°F., uncovered, for about 1 hour or until chicken is tender.

Yield: 8 servings
Per Serving:
   292 cal, 10 gm fat, 35 gm pro, 12 gm carb, 80 mg chol, 805 mg sodium, 2 gm dietary fiber

A fast food chicken dinner contains
approximately 2000 mg of sodium.

Spanish Chicken and Rice

Nutrition Staff

12 oz. skinless chicken
   breast strips
2 tsp. olive oil
1 tsp. salt-free spice/
   herb blend
1/2 c. onion, chopped
1/2 c. green bell pepper,
   chopped
2 tsp. minced garlic

1/4 tsp. cumin
1/4 tsp. pepper
1/2 c. tomato sauce
1/2 c. chicken broth
1/2 c. water
1 1/2 tsp. lemon juice
1 1/3 c. cooked rice
1 T. parsley
2 tsp. sugar

1. Wash chicken; drain.
2. Select a large nonstick skillet and heat oil over medium heat.
3. Add chicken. Sprinkle with spice/herb blend; cook and stir for about 5 minutes until chicken is lightly browned.
4. Remove chicken from skillet and set aside.
5. Combine onion, green pepper, garlic, cumin and pepper; cook and stir for 3 to 5 minutes until tender.
6. Combine tomato sauce, chicken broth, water, lemon juice and sugar; bring mixture to a boil.
7. Stir in rice and chicken pieces; cover. Remove from heat.
8. Let stand for 5 minutes; remove cover and stir in parsley.

Yield: 4 servings
Per Serving (1 cup):
   240 cal, 5 gm fat, 23 gm pro, 26 gm carb, 54 mg chol, 334 mg sodium, 2 gm dietary fiber

Limit sodium intake to less than 4000 mg a day.

Italian Chicken

Nutrition Staff

6 (4 oz.) boneless, skinless
   chicken breasts
3 T. flour
1 T. olive oil
2 T. onion, minced
1/2 tsp. minced garlic
1/2 to 3/4 c. water

1 c. tomato sauce, low-
   sodium
1/2 tsp. rosemary
1/4 tsp. pepper
1/2 tsp. basil
1/2 tsp. oregano

1. Wash chicken pieces; pat dry.
2. On a sheet of wax paper, dredge chicken in flour.
3. In a 10-inch nonstick skillet, heat oil over medium heat until hot.
4. Add chicken and cook 3 to 5 minutes on each side, turning occasionally until lightly browned on all sides.
5. Using tongs or slotted spoon, remove chicken from skillet; set aside.
6. In same skillet, sauté onion and garlic until softened.
7. Add water, tomato sauce and seasonings. Using a wooden spoon, stir well.
8. Cook, stirring frequently, until liquid is reduced by half (about 3 to 4 minutes).
9. Return chicken to skillet; cook until sauce thickens and chicken is heated through (about 1 to 2 minutes).

Yield: 6 servings
Per Serving:
   191 cal, 5 gm fat, 27 gm pro, 7 gm carb, 72 mg chol, 71 mg sodium, 1 gm dietary fiber

Neighborhood Chicken

Mary Ellen England, R.D.

4 (4 oz.) boneless, skinless
chicken breasts
1/4 c. low-calorie Italian
salad dressing
1/2 c. Italian-flavored bread
crumbs

1 T. Parmesan cheese
1 tsp. garlic powder
Nonstick vegetable
cooking spray

1. Preheat oven to 350°F.
2. With a meat mallet, pound the chicken breasts to 1/4-inch thickness.
3. Mix bread crumbs, cheese and garlic in a dish.
4. Dip the chicken in salad dressing; then dredge in crumb mixture.
5. Place chicken in a 9x9x2-inch baking dish that has been sprayed with cooking spray; bake for 20 minutes.

Yield: 4 servings
Per Serving:
200 cal, 5 gm fat, 28 gm pro, 9 gm carb, 74 mg chol, 226 mg sodium, 0 gm dietary fiber

*To increase fiber, add unprocessed bran to soups,
beverages, cooked cereals, stews, etc.*

Baked Chicken with Brown Rice and Nut Dressing

Nutrition Staff

6 (4 oz.) boneless, skinless
   chicken breasts
1 c. brown rice, uncooked
2 1/2 c. chicken broth
1/2 T. margarine or olive oil
1 c. onion, chopped

1 c. celery, chopped
1 clove garlic, minced
1 tsp. salt-free spice/
   herb blend
Pepper, to taste
1/3 c. walnuts, chopped

1. Preheat oven to 350°F.
2. Bake chicken breasts in pan covered with foil, about 45 minutes to 1 hour.
3. Remove foil last 15 minutes to brown.
4. Combine rice and chicken broth in saucepan; bring to a boil.
5. Stir once; reduce heat, cover, and simmer 45 minutes.
6. Melt margarine in saucepan.
7. Sauté onion, celery and garlic until tender.
8. Stir cooked onion, celery and garlic into cooked rice; add spice/herb blend, pepper and walnuts.
9. Serve with chicken.

Yield: 6 servings.
Per Serving:
   331 cal, 9 gm fat, 32 gm pro, 28 gm carb, 73 mg chol, 418 mg sodium, 2 gm dietary fiber

*Sedentary living may significantly lower
your HDL (good) cholesterol.*

Curried Chicken with Fruit

Veronica Coronado

1 T. margarine	1/4 tsp. salt
4 (4 oz.) boneless, skinless chicken breasts	1/4 c. raisins
1 tsp. curry powder	1 (17 oz.) can fruit cocktail in its own juice, well- drained
1/4 c. dry white wine; or dry sherry	2 T. brown sugar

1. Heat margarine in a skillet over medium heat.
2. Add chicken breasts; sauté until lightly golden on both sides.
3. While sautéing chicken, stir curry powder into margarine; add wine, salt and raisins.
4. Cover and simmer slowly over low heat about 5 minutes.
5. To test doneness, prick with a fork; juices should run clear. Do not overcook.
6. Place chicken breasts on a plate and cover loosely with skillet lid to keep warm.
7. Quickly add fruit cocktail and brown sugar to pan juices; bring to a boil and cook until syrupy.
8. Place chicken breasts on plates; pour sauce over.

Yield: 4 servings
Per Serving:
268 cal, 6 gm fat, 27 gm pro, 24 gm carb, 72 mg chol, 238 mg sodium, 2 gm dietary fiber

Choose reduced-fat cheese with 5 grams
of fat or less per 1 ounce.

Almond Chicken

Sandi Hanson

1 T. margarine	1/2 c. evaporated skimmed
8 (4 oz.) chicken breasts	milk
1/4 c. onion, chopped	2 (4 oz.) cans sliced mush-
2 T. all-purpose flour	rooms, drained
1/4 tsp. pepper	1/4 c. slivered almonds,
1 3/4 c. chicken broth	toasted
	3 c. cooked brown rice

1. In a large skillet, melt margarine. Add chicken.
2. Cover skillet. Brown chicken 10 minutes over medium heat.
3. Turn chicken and continue cooking 10 minutes.
4. Remove chicken. Add onions to skillet and sauté until lightly browned.
5. Add flour and pepper. Stir. Gradually add broth and milk; stir until thickened.
6. Return chicken breasts to skillet; add 1 can mushrooms.
7. Heat, without boiling, 15 to 20 minutes; stir frequently.
8. Combine toasted almonds and second can of mushrooms with cooked rice. Serve chicken breasts over rice.

Yield: 8 servings
Per Serving:
    309 cal, 8 gm fat, 32 gm pro, 26 gm carb, 73 mg chol, 405 mg sodium, 3 gm dietary fiber

Regular exercise lowers blood lipids (fats),
blood pressure and reduces stress.

Lemon Chicken
Cindy Wachtler, R.D.

6 (4 oz.) boneless, skinless chicken breasts	1 1/2 tsp. vegetable oil
Juice of 1 lemon	1 T. water
1/4 tsp. ginger	1 head of broccoli, cut up
1/2 tsp. minced garlic	1 T. vegetable oil
2 T. cornstarch	1/8 tsp. pepper
	1 c. chicken broth

1. Cut chicken into thin strips; put into bowl.
2. Add lemon juice, ginger, garlic, cornstarch, 1 1/2 teaspoon oil and water; combine all these ingredients and marinate 10 minutes.
3. Heat the 1 tablespoon oil in a heavy skillet. When oil is very hot, add broccoli; season with pepper stirring constantly for 2 minutes.
4. Remove broccoli; set aside.
5. Add marinated chicken to the hot skillet, stirring constantly for about 3 minutes.
6. Add chicken broth; bring to a boil.
7. Add reserved broccoli; combine and serve.

Yield: 6 servings
Per Serving:
> 219 cal, 7 gm fat, 31 gm pro, 9 gm carb, 72 mg chol, 203 mg sodium, 3 gm dietary fiber

Lemon Baked Chicken
Nutrition Staff

1 (2 1/2 to 3 lb.) chicken, cut into serving pieces & skin removed	1 tsp. minced garlic
	2 tsp. oregano
	1/8 tsp. pepper
1 T. lemon juice	Fresh parsley sprigs to
1 T. olive oil	garnish (optional)

1. Wash chicken pieces; pat dry and set aside.
2. In a bowl, combine lemon juice, olive oil, garlic, oregano and pepper. Arrange chicken in a shallow baking pan, and pour the lemon mixture on top.
3. Cover and bake in 350°F. oven until tender, about 40 minutes, basting occasionally. Uncover and bake 10 minutes longer to allow chicken to brown. Serve with parsley sprigs.

Yield: 4 servings
Per Serving:
> 206 cal, 9 gm fat, 28 gm pro, 1 gm carb, 85 mg chol, 79 mg sodium, 0 gm dietary fiber

Apricot Chicken

Kerry and Tom Siekmann

3/4 c. wild rice, uncooked
1/2 c. brown rice, uncooked
2 (8 oz.) cans apricot nectar
6 (4 oz.) boneless, skinless
  chicken breasts

1 c. apricot halves, canned
  in light syrup
1/2 tsp. salt
1 tsp. rosemary

1. Place rice in bottom of 9x13x2-inch casserole dish.
2. Add 1 can of apricot nectar to rice. Sprinkle with salt.
3. Place chicken breasts on rice.
4. Add second can of apricot nectar just until casserole dish is full (leave about 1/4 to 1/2 inch empty so it doesn't boil over).
5. Place apricot halves on top of chicken breasts. Sprinkle with rosemary.
6. Cover with foil and bake at 350°F. for about 1 1/2 hours or until rice is done. You may want to place a cookie sheet under the casserole dish before baking, in case it does boil over.

Yield: 6 servings
Per Serving:
   325 cal, 4 gm fat, 31 gm pro, 41 gm carb, 72 mg chol, 248 mg sodium, 3 gm dietary fiber

Life Saver Chicken

Susan Hoobler

7 (4 oz.) chicken breasts
1/2 (8 oz.) btl. sweet & spicy
  French or Russian
  dressing, low-calorie

1 (8 oz.) can cranberry
  sauce with whole
  cranberries
1/2 pkg. onion soup mix,
  dry

1. Mix all ingredients, except chicken, together.
2. Put chicken in baking dish and pour sauce over it.
3. Bake at 350°F. for 45 minutes or microwave on high for 20 minutes.

Yield: 7 servings
Per Serving:
   213 cal, 4 gm fat, 27 gm pro, 17 gm carb, 73 chol, 244 mg sodium, 0 mg dietary fiber

10-Minute Chicken

Nutrition Staff

4 (4 oz.) skinless chicken breasts	1 tsp. salt-free spice/ herb blend
3 T. lemon juice	1/2 tsp. paprika

1. Wash chicken pieces; pat dry.
2. Arrange chicken breasts in a microwavable pan, with thick pieces to the outside, thin pieces toward the center. Sprinkle with lemon juice and seasonings.
3. Cover and microwave on high for 7 minutes. Rotate pan at least once during cooking. Check for doneness (juice runs clear when meat is pierced with a fork).

NOTE: Cooking time must be reduced if fewer pieces are used.

Yield: 4 servings
Per Serving:
146 cal, 3 gm fat, 27 gm pro, 1 gm carb, 72 mg chol, 62 mg sodium, 0 gm dietary fiber

Chicken and Vegetables Cooked in Foil

Veronica Coronado

4 (4 oz.) boneless, skinless chicken breasts	4 tsp. margarine
2 carrots, cut into 1" slices	2 T. cooking sherry
8 oz. fresh mushrooms, sliced 1/4" thick	1/4 tsp. pepper
1 c. zucchini, sliced	1/4 tsp. seasoned salt
	2 tsp. rosemary

1. Preheat oven to 350°F.
2. Tear off four 12-inch pieces of foil.
3. Place 1 chicken breast on each piece of foil.
4. Cover each piece of chicken with vegetables, margarine, sherry and seasonings, dividing ingredients equally.
5. Fold foil around each breast to make a tight pouch.
6. Place foil package on a cookie sheet: bake for 30 to 40 minutes.

Yield: 4 servings
Per Serving:
224 cal, 7 gm fat, 28 gm pro, 8 gm carb, 72 mg chol, 253 mg sodium, 2 gm dietary fiber

Stir-Fried Chicken

Nutrition Staff

**16 oz. chicken breast
strips**
1 T. olive oil
1/2 tsp. minced garlic

1/2 tsp. ginger
2 T. light soy sauce

USE FRESH VEGETABLES:
**2 med. carrots, peeled &
julienne sliced**
OR USE:
**1 (16 oz.) pkg. frozen plain
vegetable combination**

2 c. broccoli pieces
1 stalk celery, chopped

1. Wash chicken pieces; pat dry.
2. Add olive oil to electric skillet or wok; add garlic and ginger.
3. Heat skillet or wok on medium-high setting; stir-fry chicken for about 5 minutes tossing every few minutes to assure that all pieces brown evenly.
4. Add vegetables and 1 to 2 tablespoons water; stir-fry vegetables another 3 minutes.
5. Add 2 tablespoons soy sauce during last 2 minutes of cooking.

Yield: 4 servings
Per Serving (3 ounces chicken, 3/4 cup vegetables):
203 cal, 7 gm fat, 29 gm pro, 7 gm carb, 72 mg chol, 393 mg sodium, 2 gm dietary fiber

*Maintain a healthy diet of 30% calories from
fat (50-70 grams of fat daily).*

Chicken Fajitas

Cindy Kleckner, R.D.

2 to 2 1/4 lb. boneless, skinless chicken fillets

MARINADE:

3 T. white wine
1 1/2 T. margarine
1 T. light soy sauce

1 T. minced garlic
1 tsp. pepper (adjust to
   desired taste)

FAJITAS:

1 T. lime juice
1 c. onion, sliced

1 green bell pepper, sliced
13 (6") flour tortillas

1. Combine marinade ingredients in a pan; marinate chicken. Reserve marinade.
2. Grill marinated chicken; cut into strips and squeeze lime juice over top.
3. In a nonstick skillet sauté onions and green peppers in 3 tablespoons of marinade.
4. Combine chicken, onions and green pepper and serve with warmed tortillas.

Yield: 13 servings
Per Serving (1 fajita):
   188 cal, 4 gm fat, 20 gm pro, 16 gm carb, 47 mg chol, 217 mg sodium,
   1 gm dietary fiber

Evaporated skimmed milk is a "creamy"
low-calorie, low-fat alternative to cream.

Grilled Sesame Chicken Breasts

Nutrition Staff

**4 (4 oz.) boneless, skinless
   chicken breasts**
1/2 c. white grape juice
1/4 c. light soy sauce

1 T. sesame seeds
2 T. sesame oil
1/4 tsp. garlic powder
1/4 tsp. ginger

1. Wash chicken pieces; pat dry. Set aside.
2. Combine all ingredients except chicken in a shallow pan (or zip-lock bag); mix well.
3. Add chicken pieces, turning to coat; cover and marinate in refrigerator at least 4 hours.
4. Remove chicken from marinade, reserving marinade.
5. Grill 4 to 5 inches from medium-hot coals for 12 to 15 minutes, turning and basting frequently with marinade.

Yield: 4 servings
Per Serving:
   176 cal, 6 gm fat, 27 gm pro, 2 gm carb, 72 mg chol, 262 mg sodium, 0 gm dietary fiber

Garlic Grilled Chicken

Carole Kerby

**4 (4 oz.) boneless, skinless
   chicken breasts**
1 c. picante sauce
1 T. lime juice
2 cloves garlic, minced

1/2 tsp. cumin
**1/2 tsp. whole oregano,
   diced & crushed**
1/4 tsp. salt
3/4 c. picante sauce

1. Mix all ingredients except chicken and 3/4 cup picante sauce; marinate chicken in marinade for a minimum of 1 1/2 hours.
2. Pour off marinade; grill on outdoor or indoor grill.
3. Heat 3/4 cup picante sauce; drizzle over chicken just before serving.

Yield: 4 servings
Per Serving:
   167 cal, 5 gm fat, 27 gm pro, 5 gm carb, 72 mg chol, 390 mg sodium, 0 gm dietary fiber

Grilled Dijon Chicken

Patty Kirk, R.D.

4 (4 oz.) skinless chicken
   breasts
2 tsp. Dijon-style mustard
1/4 tsp. pepper

5 tsp. diet margarine
2 tsp. lemon juice
1/2 tsp. minced garlic
1 tsp. tarragon

1. Wash chicken pieces; pat dry.
2. Spread mustard on both sides of chicken and sprinkle with pepper; cover and refrigerate 4 hours.
3. Melt margarine and stir in lemon juice, garlic and tarragon.
4. Place chicken on grill; baste with sauce. Grill 40 to 45 minutes or until done, turning and basting frequently.

Yield: 4 servings
Per Serving:
   165 cal, 5 gm fat, 27 gm pro, 1 gm carb, 72 mg chol, 157 mg sodium, 0 gm dietary fiber

Chili, Chicken Stew

Tony York

6 (4 oz.) boneless, skinless
   chicken breasts
1 c. onion, chopped
1 green bell pepper,
   chopped
1 tsp. minced garlic
1 T. vegetable oil

2 (14 1/2 oz.) cans stewed
   tomatoes, chopped
1 (15 oz.) can pinto beans,
   drained
3/4 c. picante sauce
1 tsp. chili powder
1 tsp. cumin

1. Cut chicken into 1-inch pieces; cook chicken, onion, green pepper and garlic in oil in Dutch oven or skillet until chicken loses its pink color.
2. Add remaining ingredients; simmer 2 to 3 hours.
3. May serve over brown rice and top with 1 tablespoon grated low-fat cheese and chopped green onion.

Yield: 6 servings
Per Serving:
   324 cal, 7 gm fat, 35 gm pro, 32 gm carb, 72 mg chol, 528 mg sodium, 7 gm dietary fiber

Crockpot Chicken

Veronica Coronado

3 lb. chicken, cut into
   serving pieces and skinned
1/2 tsp. garlic salt
1/2 tsp. pepper
1 tsp. cinnamon
1 green bell pepper,
   seeded & chopped
2 sm. onions, sliced
2 stalks celery, chopped

1 (4 oz.) can sliced mushrooms, drained
1/4 c. dry sherry
1 (16 oz.) can tomato
   wedges
3 T. flour
3 T. water
16 oz. spaghetti, cooked

1. Rinse chicken pieces; pat dry.
2. Season with garlic salt, pepper and cinnamon.
3. Place green pepper, onions and celery in crockpot.
4. Add seasoned chicken pieces; pour in mushrooms, sherry and tomatoes.
5. Stir well.
6. Cover and cook on low setting for 8 to 10 hours.
7. Remove chicken pieces with spoon; debone and return meat to sauce.
8. Make a smooth paste of flour and water; stir into crockpot.
9. Cover and cook on high setting for 15 to 30 minutes or until gravy is
   thickened.
10. Serve over hot spaghetti.

Yield: 8 servings
Per Serving (1 1/2 cups):
   380 cal, 6 gm fat, 28 gm pro, 50 gm carb, 61 mg chol, 365 mg sodium,
   4 gm dietary fiber

*You need a minimum of 8 cups of fluid
daily ... 4 of which are water.*

Quick Turkey Spaghetti
Tricia Cox

1 onion, chopped
1 T. diet margarine
1 (14 1/2 oz.) can
   tomatoes, chopped
1 can creamy chicken &
   mushroom soup

1 c. part-skim mozzarella
   cheese, grated
2 1/2 c. cooked turkey,
   chopped
8 oz. dry spaghetti
Pepper, to taste

1. Sauté onion in margarine.
2. Stir in tomatoes, soup and turkey; season to taste with pepper; simmer.
3. Cook spaghetti according to package directions.
4. Drain spaghetti and mix with sauce.
5. Put half of mixture in baking dish; cover with half of the cheese.
6. Repeat #5 and bake in preheated oven at 350°F. covered for 20 to 30 minutes.

Yield: 8 servings
Per Serving:
   275 cal, 9 gm fat, 22 gm pro, 27 gm carb, 41 mg chol, 500 mg sodium, 2 gm dietary fiber

Broiled Chicken Breast Sandwiches
Cindy Kleckner, R.D.

1/4 c. light soy sauce
1 clove garlic, minced
1/2 T. sugar
2 T. fresh ginger, minced; or
   1/4 to 1/2 tsp. ginger
   powder
1/2 c. orange or pineapple
   juice

1 T. olive oil
1/4 c. sherry
4 (4 oz.) boneless, skin-
   less chicken breasts
4 wholewheat buns
4 lettuce leaves
1 tomato (8 slices)

1. Blend all ingredients; marinate chicken breasts for 3 hours.
2. Broil or grill chicken breasts, basting while cooking.
3. Serve on buns with lettuce and tomato.

Yield: 4 servings
Per Serving (1 sandwich):
   308 cal, 6 gm fat, 32 gm pro, 29 gm carb, 72 mg chol, 522 mg sodium, 4 gm dietary fiber

Picnic Chicken Salad Sandwiches

Cindy Wachtler, R.D.

2 c. cooked chicken breast, chopped
1 med. Granny Smith apple, chopped
1/2 c. celery, chopped
1/3 c. green onions, thinly sliced
1/4 c. plain nonfat yogurt
1/4 c. low-fat mayonnaise

1/4 c. water chestnuts, chopped
2 T. fresh parsley, chopped
2 tsp. lemon juice
1/2 tsp. pepper
1/4 tsp. salt
8 lettuce leaves
8 wholewheat pita pockets

1. Combine all salad ingredients in a medium bowl and chill.
2. Line each pocket with a lettuce leaf and fill with 1/2 cup chicken salad.

Yield: 8 servings
Per Serving (1 pocket sandwich):
276 cal, 5 gm fat, 19 gm pro, 39 gm carb, 34 mg chol, 473 mg sodium, 5 gm dietary fiber

Notes and Recipes

Sensational
Seafood

Sensational Seafood

Sensational Seafood

Blackened Fish Fillets   Jean Wisner, R.D.

1 lg. 12 oz. fish fillet	1 tsp. paprika
(orange roughy, trout,	1/8 tsp. garlic powder
redfish)	1/8 tsp. onion powder
1/4 tsp. salt	2 tsp. olive oil
1/2 tsp. cayenne pepper	Nonstick vegetable
1/2 tsp. pepper	cooking spray

1. Coat a nonstick skillet with cooking spray.
2. Place skillet on high heat.
3. Cut fish fillet in 3 pieces; pat moisture from fish in paper towels.
4. In a medium bowl, blend salt, cayenne pepper, paprika, garlic powder and onion powder.
5. Dredge fillets in seasoning blend.
6. Add oil to skillet; add fillets.
7. Cook 3 to 4 minutes on each side.

Yield: 3 servings
Per Serving:
   140 cal, 5 gm fat, 23 gm pro, 1 gm carb, 40 mg chol, 227 mg sodium, 0 gm dietary fiber

Sprinkle-on butter flavorings contain
only 4 calories per 1/2 teaspoon.

Fish with Fruit Salsa
Cindy Kleckner, R.D.

1/2 sm. ripe papaya, peeled,
    seeded & chopped
1 sm. ripe nectarine, pitted
    & chopped
1 fresh jalapeño pepper,
    seeded & chopped

1 tsp. basil
4 tsp. olive oil, divided
4 fresh or frozen halibut
    (approx. 2 lb.)
Nonstick vegetable
    cooking spray

1. Thaw fish if frozen.
2. Several hours ahead, for fruit salsa, stir together the papaya, nectarine, jalapeño pepper, basil and 2 teaspoons olive oil; cover and chill thoroughly.
3. Spray grill rack with cooking spray.
4. Brush both sides of steaks with 1 teaspoon olive oil; grill fish on an uncovered grill until fish flakes with a fork.
5. Allow 4 to 6 minutes cooking time for each 1/2-inch thickness.
6. Turn fish halfway through cooking time, and brush again with olive oil.
7. Serve fish with the fruit salsa.

Yield: 4 servings.
Per Serving (1 steak):
    303 cal, 10 gm fat, 46 gm pro, 6 gm carb, 70 mg chol, 149 mg sodium, 1 gm dietary fiber

Crispy Broiled Fish
Kathryn Miller, M.S., R.D.

1 egg white
1/4 tsp. salt
Dash of pepper
1 1/2 tsp. lemon juice

1/2 c. cornflakes, finely
    crushed
8 oz. orange roughy
Nonstick vegetable
    cooking spray

1. Heat oven to 350°F.
2. In a small bowl, combine the first 4 ingredients; mix well.
3. Dip fish in egg mixture, then coat with cornflake crumbs.
4. Spray the bottom of a broiling pan with cooking spray.
5. Arrange fish in pan.
6. Broil uncovered for 10 minutes (8 inches from heat source).

Yield: 2 servings
Per Serving:
    132 cal, 1 gm fat, 23 gm pro, 7 gm carb, 58 mg chol, 462 gm sodium, 0 gm dietary fiber

Garlic-Herb Fillets

Nutrition Staff

1 T. water
1 tsp. orange peel, grated
1/2 tsp. rosemary
1/4 tsp. thyme
1/2 tsp. minced garlic

1 T. dried parsley
16 oz. fish fillets, about
1/2" thick, cut into 4
serving-size pieces

1. In a small bowl, combine water, orange peel, rosemary, thyme and garlic. Cover with plastic wrap.
2. Microwave on high for 1 minute; stir in parsley.
3. Arrange fillets in a 9-inch square baking dish with thickest portions toward outside of dish; top with parsley mixture.
4. Cover with wax paper; microwave at high for 5 to 7 minutes, or until fish flakes easily with fork, rotating dish once.
5. Let stand, covered, for 3 minutes.

Yield: 4 servings
Per Serving:
104 cal, 1 gm fat, 21 gm pro, 1 gm carb, 58 mg chol, 93 mg sodium, 0 gm dietary fiber

Parmesan Broiled Fish

Kathryn Miller, M.S.,R.D.

1 lb. orange roughy
1 T. Dijon-style mustard
1 T. lemon juice
2 T. grated Parmesan cheese

1/3 c. plain nonfat yogurt
Lemon wedges & dill sprigs
to garnish

1. Arrange fish fillets on a broiler pan.
2. Combine mustard, lemon juice, Parmesan cheese and yogurt in a small bowl. Spread the mixture over the fillets in a thin layer.
3. Broil about 8 inches from heat for about 10 minutes, or until fish flakes easily.
4. Garnish with lemon and dill.

Yield: 4 servings
Per Serving:
126 cal, 2 gm fat, 23 gm pro, 2 gm carb, 60 chol, 199 mg sodium, 0 gm dietary fiber

Portuguese Cod

Nutrition Staff

2 tsp. olive oil, divided
1/4 c. onion, diced
1/2 tsp. minced garlic
1/2 c. green bell pepper,
    diced
3/4 c. unsalted canned
    tomatoes, crushed
2 T. white wine

4 pitted black olives,
    sliced
12 oz. cod fillets (three
    4 oz. fillets)
1/4 tsp. salt
1/2 tsp. pepper
2 tsp. fresh parsley

1. In a 1-quart saucepan, heat 1 teaspoon oil; add onion and garlic. Sauté until onion is softened.
2. Add green pepper; sauté for 3 minutes longer.
3. Add tomatoes, wine and olives; cover and let simmer for 10 minutes. Stir occasionally.
4. Sprinkle both sides of cod fillets with salt and pepper.
5. In a 9-inch skillet, heat remaining 1 teaspoon oil; add fish and cook for 3 to 4 minutes.
6. Turn fish and top with vegetable mixture; let simmer approximately 3 minutes until fish flakes easily when tested with a fork and vegetables are hot.
7. Transfer to platter and garnish with fresh parsley.

Yield: 3 servings
Per Serving:
153 cal, 5 gm fat, 20 gm pro, 5 gm carb, 47 mg chol, 303 mg sodium, 2 gm dietary fiber

One 3-ounce serving of fried fish contains
approximately 194 calories and 11 grams of fat.

Orange Roughy with Cheese Crumb Topping

Cindy Kleckner, R.D.

1 lb. orange roughy fillets
1/2 T. diet margarine
1/2 onion, finely chopped
1/2 tsp. minced garlic
3/4 c. Italian-flavored
    bread crumbs

1/4 c. part-skim mozzarella
    cheese, finely grated
1 tsp. paprika
Pepper, to taste
Nonstick vegetable
    cooking spray

1. Preheat oven to 350°F.
2. Spray ovenproof dish with cooking spray; place fish in prepared dish.
3. Melt margarine; add onion and garlic. Cook until onion is soft.
4. Transfer to bowl and toss with bread crumbs, cheese and paprika; season to taste with pepper.
5. Spoon mixture evenly over fish.
6. Bake until fish flakes and crumb topping is golden, about 15 to 20 minutes.

Yield: 4 servings
Per Serving:
   197 cal, 4 gm fat, 25 gm pro, 14 gm carb, 62 mg chol, 268 mg sodium, 1 gm dietary fiber

Citrus Orange Roughy

Veronica Coronado

1/4 c. orange juice
4 (6 oz.) orange roughy fillets
1 T. olive oil

1 T. tarragon
3/4 tsp. pepper
Grated zest of 2 oranges

1. Preheat oven to 325°F.
2. Pour the orange juice into a shallow baking dish large enough to hold the fish in one layer.
3. Brush the fish lightly with oil on both sides and place the fillets in the baking dish.
4. Combine the tarragon, pepper and orange zest in a small bowl; sprinkle over the fish, patting it lightly to form a thin crust.
5. Bake until the fish flakes easily with a fork, 20 to 25 minutes.
6. Using a long metal spatula, carefully transfer the fish to a serving dish. (The fish may release a lot of liquid while cooking; just discard it.)
7. Serve immediately.

Yield: 4 servings
Per Serving (1 fillet):
   122 cal, 4 gm fat, 21 gm pro, 1 gm carb, 58 mg chol, 90 mg sodium, 0 gm dietary fiber

Orange Roughy with Confetti Fruit

Jean Wisner, R.D.

1 1/2 lb. orange roughy
fillets

Nonstick vegetable
cooking spray

CONFETTI FRUIT:

1 1/2 c. fresh fruit, diced
(any combination of
pineapple, papaya,
mango, melon, kiwi,
peach)

1/3 c. red bell pepper, diced

1 1/2 T. cilantro, chopped
1 T. lime or lemon juice
1/4 tsp. minced garlic
Generous pinch of hot red
pepper flakes

1. Rinse fish; pat dry with paper towels.
2. Cut fish into 4 equal portions.
3. Spray fish generously with cooking spray.
4. Grill fish over hot coals 7 minutes on each side, or microwave on high 10 to 12 minutes until fish flakes easily.
5. Serve with confetti fruit.

Yield: 4 servings
Per Serving:
182 cal, 2 gm fat, 31 gm pro, 8 gm carb, 87 mg chol, 138 mg sodium, 1 gm dietary fiber

BAKED FISH:
To keep fish from sticking to the pan, bake on a bed of chopped onion, celery and parsley. This also adds a nice flavor to the fish.

Salmon with Spring Sauce

Kathy Duran, R.D.

3 tsp. lemon juice
Lemon zest of 1 lemon (1 T.)
1 tsp. thyme
4 (4 oz.) skinless salmon
  fillets
1/4 c. onion, finely chopped
1/4 red bell pepper, peeled
  or skin steamed off,
  diced into 1/4" pieces
2 radishes, cut into match-
  sticks

1 T. capers, rinsed &
  drained
1 scallion, minced; or 1
  clove garlic
1 T. parsley
1/8 tsp. salt
1/8 tsp. pepper
1/2 T. lemon juice
1 tsp. cornstarch
2 tsp. water
Nonstick vegetable
  cooking spray

1. In a small bowl, combine lemon juice, lemon zest and thyme.
2. Arrange salmon in shallow dish and spray with cooking spray.
3. Sprinkle lemon juice and thyme mixture over the top; cover and refrigerate for about 2 hours.
4. Soak onion in cold water for 5 minutes; drain.
5. In a medium bowl, combine onion, red bell pepper, radishes, capers, scallions and parsley; set aside.
6. In a large, nonstick skillet, arrange salmon fillets in a single layer; sprinkle with salt and pepper and add 1/2 cup water.
7. Cover and bring to a boil; boil approximately 3 minutes.
8. By the time the water boils, the bottom side of salmon will be done.
9. Using a spatula, turn salmon fillets over and return to a boil.
10. Reduce heat, cover and cook until salmon is barely opaque in the center, about 1 1/2 minutes.
11. Drain juices into a small skillet; keep salmon covered and set aside.
12. Bring reserved juices to a boil; add the 1/2 tablespoon lemon juice.
13. Return to a boil.
14. Mix cornstarch with water to form a paste; add cornstarch paste to boiling juices (to thicken) and whisk.
15. Remove from heat and stir in reserved vegetables; spoon sauce over salmon and serve.

Yield: 4 servings
Per Serving:
175 cal, 7 gm fat, 24 gm pro, 4 gm carb, 51 mg chol, 127 mg sodium, 0 gm dietary fiber

Salmon Croquettes

Nutrition Staff

1 (15 1/2 oz.) can salmon,
   drained & flaked
2 T. onion, grated
4 egg whites, beaten until
   frothy & divided

1/8 tsp. pepper
1/4 tsp. salt
1/2 c. bread crumbs

1. Place salmon in a colander and drain for 1 minute.
2. Combine salmon, onion, 2 beaten egg whites, salt, pepper and 1/2 of bread crumbs; stir well.
3. Divide mixture into 6 equal portions.
4. Dip each croquette in remaining egg white mixture and then in remaining bread crumbs.
5. Bake croquettes in preheated 350°F. oven for 25 to 30 minutes or until crust is brown.

Yield: 6 servings
Per Serving (1 croquette):
   146 cal, 5 gm fat, 17 gm pro, 6 gm carb, 31 mg chol, 551 mg sodium, 0 gm dietary fiber

Increase calcium in your diet by choosing yogurts
with 5 grams of fat or less per 8-ounce serving.

Shrimp Jambalaya

Cindy Kleckner, R.D.

3/4 lb. (31/35 count) un-
  cooked shrimp, peeled
  & deveined
3/4 c. onion, finely chopped
1 clove garlic, minced
1 T. diet margarine
2 whole cloves
4 T. tomato paste
1/4 c. celery, finely chopped
1/8 c. green bell pepper,
  finely chopped

1/2 T. parsley
1 (14 1/2 oz.) can
  tomatoes, undrained
1/4 tsp. thyme
1/4 tsp. cayenne pepper
1/8 tsp. freshly ground
  pepper
3 c. cooked rice

1. Boil shrimp until pink, about 5 minutes; drain and set aside.
2. Sauté onion and garlic in margarine in a nonstick skillet for a few minutes.
3. Add tomatoes and tomato paste, stirring to chop tomatoes; cook 5 minutes.
4. Add all ingredients except shrimp and rice; cook 5 minutes.
5. Add shrimp and rice; stir over low heat until mixture is dry.
6. Serve immediately.

Yield: 6 servings
Per Serving:
  182 cal, 2 gm fat, 10 gm pro, 33 gm carb, 43 mg chol, 214 mg sodium, 2 gm dietary fiber

The odor from baking or broiling salmon may be eliminated by squeezing lemon juice on both sides of each salmon steak or on the cut surface of the salmon, and letting it stand in the refrigerator for one hour before cooking.

Hot and Sour Shrimp
Veronica Coronado

1 lb. lg. uncooked shrimp, peeled, deveined & butterflied
4 T. sherry
1 T. fresh ginger, peeled & grated
1/2 c. chicken stock or canned broth
2 T. light soy sauce
2 T. ketchup
1 T. cornstarch
1 T. rice vinegar or white wine vinegar
1 T. sugar

1 tsp. oriental sesame oil
1/4 tsp. cayenne pepper
3 1/2 tsp. peanut oil, divided
2 T. walnuts, chopped
4 bunches watercress, trimmed
2 med. red bell peppers, cut into 1" squares
2 garlic cloves, minced
8 green onions, cut diagonally into 1" long pieces
Nonstick vegetable cooking spray

1. Combine shrimp, 2 tablespoons sherry and ginger in large bowl; cover and refrigerate for 30 minutes.
2. Mix remaining 2 tablespoons sherry, chicken stock, soy sauce, ketchup, cornstarch, vinegar, sugar, sesame oil and cayenne pepper in a small bowl.
3. Spray wok or heavy large skillet with cooking spray; heat 1 teaspoon peanut oil on high.
4. Add walnuts and stir-fry 1 minute.
5. Transfer walnuts to plate using slotted spoon.
6. Add watercress to wok and stir-fry until just wilted, about 1 minute.
7. Divide watercress among 4 plates.
8. Add 1 1/2 teaspoons peanut oil, red pepper and garlic to wok; stir-fry 1 minute.
9. Add remaining 1 teaspoon peanut oil, shrimp mixture and onions; stir-fry 1 minute.
10. Stir stock mixture, add to wok and cook sauce until clear and thick, stirring frequently, 2 minutes.
11. Spoon sauce and shrimp over watercress.
12. Sprinkle with walnuts and serve.

Yield: 4 servings
Per Serving:
206 cal, 8 gm fat, 15 gm pro, 16 gm carb, 82 mg chol, 617 mg sodium, 2 gm dietary fiber

Shrimp Creole
Georgia Kostas, M.P.H., R.D.

1/2 c. onion, diced
1/2 c. celery, diced
1/2 c. green bell pepper, diced
1/2 tsp. minced garlic
2 T. diet margarine

2 (8 oz.) cans tomato sauce
1/8 tsp. pepper
1/4 tsp. chili powder
1 lb. sm. shrimp, cooked,
   peeled & cut in pieces
4 c. cooked rice

1. Melt margarine in skillet; sauté vegetables and garlic in melted margarine.
2. Blend together tomato sauce, pepper and chili powder.
3. Add tomato mixture to vegetables and simmer for 15 minutes.
4. Add cooked shrimp and heat thoroughly.
5. Serve over cooked rice.

Yield: 6 servings
Per Serving:
   233 cal, 2 gm fat, 12 gm pro, 42 gm carb, 55 mg chol, 599 mg sodium, 3 gm dietary fiber

Mediterranean Shrimp with Feta Cheese
Jean Wisner, R.D.

1 lg. onion, chopped
Nonstick cooking spray
1 (16 oz.) can chopped tomatoes
1 T. fresh parsley, chopped
1 T. fresh basil, chopped,
   or 1/4 T. dry basil

2 T. tomato paste
1/2 tsp. cayenne pepper
1 tsp. minced garlic
2 lb. shrimp, peeled & deveined
6 oz. feta cheese
8 c. cooked pasta (16 oz. dry)

1. Spray a nonstick skillet with cooking spray; sauté onion.
2. Add tomatoes with juice, parsley, basil, tomato paste, cayenne pepper and garlic; cover and simmer 10 minutes.
3. Add shrimp to sauce and cook 2 to 3 minutes. If sauce is too thick add up to 3 tablespoons of water before adding shrimp.
4. Pour into a 3-quart baking dish.
5. Crumble cheese over shrimp; bake 10 to 15 minutes at 350°F. and remove from oven.
6. Serve over pasta.

Yield: 8 servings
Per Serving:
   346 cal, 6 gm fat, 22 gm pro, 49 gm carb, 101 mg chol, 461 mg sodium, 4 gm dietary fiber

Saucy Shrimp Sauté

Cindy Kleckner, R.D.

16 lg. shrimp, peeled & deveined
1 T. fresh ginger, chopped; or 1 tsp. ginger powder

2 T. green onions, chopped
2 sm. red chile peppers, chopped
1 T. vegetable oil

SEASONING:
3 T. sherry
2 T. tomato sauce or ketchup

1 1/2 T. worcestershire sauce
1 1/2 T. light soy sauce
2 T. water

1. Peel and devein shrimp; rinse with cold water and spread on paper towel to dry 10 to 12 minutes.
2. Heat oil in skillet or wok over high heat; sauté ginger and green onions for 30 seconds.
3. Add shrimp; brown each side for 1 to 1 1/2 minutes.
4. Add seasonings; stirring constantly over medium heat until sauce thickens a little and shrimp have firm texture.
5. For spicy variation, add chili pepper to taste during cooking.

Yield: 4 servings
Per Serving:
120 cal, 4 gm fat, 14 gm pro, 4 gm carb, 92 mg chol, 557 mg sodium, 0 mg dietary fiber

During cycling, drink one 20-ounce bottle of water every 5 to 10 miles to prevent dehydration.

Scallops Thermidor

Cindy Kleckner, R.D.

8 oz. scallops
1 tsp. margarine
1 tsp. lemon juice
1 T. flour
1/2 c. skim milk

1 tsp. parsley
1 T. Parmesan cheese
1/4 tsp. paprika
Nonstick vegetable
cooking spray

1. Preheat oven to 400°F.
2. Wash scallops under cold running water; pat dry.
3. Cut large scallops into bite-size pieces.
4. Melt margarine in 8-inch pan.
5. Add lemon juice and scallops; cook over low heat for 2 minutes, stirring frequently.
6. Stir in flour.
7. Add milk gradually; cook until thick and smooth, stirring constantly.
8. Add parsley.
9. Place mixture into two 6-ounce custard cups that have been sprayed with cooking spray.
10. Sprinkle with Parmesan cheese and paprika.
11. Bake 5 to 10 minutes or until lightly browned.

Yield: 2 servings
Per Serving:
162 cal, 4 gm fat, 23 gm pro, 9 gm carb, 48 mg chol, 326 mg sodium, 0 gm dietary fiber

When making crackers crumbs, put the crackers in a clear bag and use the rolling pin to crush them. This doesn't make a mess on the counter or the rolling pin and the crumbs can be easily poured from the bag into a measuring cup.

Linguine and Scallops

Nutrition Staff

7 oz. linguine, dry
8 oz. scallops, rinsed & drained
1 1/2 c. fresh mushrooms, sliced
1/3 c. green onions, sliced
1/4 c. fresh parsley, snipped

1/2 tsp. minced garlic
2 T. diet margarine
Dash of cayenne pepper (optional)
3 T. Parmesan cheese
1 T. Chablis or other dry white wine
Nonstick vegetable cooking spray

1. Cut scallops into bite-size pieces.
2. Rinse scallops in cold water; drain and set aside.
3. Coat large skillet with cooking spray; add diet margarine and place over medium-high heat until margarine melts.
4. Add mushrooms, green onions and garlic; sauté 1 minute or until tender.
5. Using a slotted spoon, remove vegetables from skillet; set aside.
6. Add scallops, wine and cayenne pepper; bring mixture to a boil. Cover and reduce heat.
7. Simmer mixture 5 to 6 minutes or until scallops are done. If more liquid is needed, add 1 to 2 tablespoons more wine.
8. Add vegetables and cook until heated.
9. Cook linguine according to directions on package.
10. Serve vegetables over linguine and sprinkle with Parmesan cheese and parsley.

Yield: 4 servings
Per Serving (1 1/2 cup):
275 cal, 5 gm fat, 18 gm pro, 38 gm carb, 25 mg chol, 261 mg sodium, 2 gm dietary fiber

You can get more juice from a dried-up lemon if you heat it for five minutes in boiling water before you squeeze it.

Red Snapper Stew

Nutrition Staff

2 tsp. vegetable oil
2 c. onion, chopped
1 c. celery, chopped
1/2 c. green bell pepper,
  chopped
1/2 tsp. minced garlic
1 1/2 c. water
1 1/2 tsp. chicken bouillon
  granules
1 c. Chablis or other dry
  white wine

1 lg. potato (1/2 lb.), cut
  into cubes
1 (14 1/2 oz.) can toma-
  toes, low-sodium,
  chopped
1/4 tsp. salt
1/4 tsp. red pepper
1 bay leaf
1 1/2 lb. skinless red
  snapper fillets

1. In a large pot, heat oil; add onion, celery, green pepper and garlic.
   Sauté until vegetables are tender.
2. Stir in water and next 7 ingredients; bring to a boil
3. Cover; reduce heat, and simmer 20 minutes.
4. Rinse fish with cold water and pat dry; cut fish into 1-inch cubes and
   add to stew.
5. Cover and simmer 10 minutes, or until fish flakes.
6. Remove and discard bay leaf. Ladle into serving bowls.

Yield: 8 servings
Per Serving (1 cup):
  172 cal, 3 gm fat, 19 gm pro, 14 gm carb, 30 mg chol, 319 mg sodium,
  3 gm dietary fiber

*To keep sour cream fresh longer, store upside down in
the refrigerator so that air cannot enter the container.*

Dilly Sauce

Cindy Kleckner, R.D.

1 T. diet margarine
1 T. onion, minced
1 T. cornstarch
1/4 tsp. salt

1/2 tsp. dill weed
1/8 tsp. pepper
1 c. skim milk
1/2 c. plain nonfat yogurt

1. In a small saucepan, melt margarine.
2. Add onion; sauté until tender.
3. In a small bowl, combine cornstarch, salt, dill weed, pepper and milk.
4. Pour into saucepan; stir.
5. Bring to a boil.
6. Cook, stirring over medium heat until thickened, about 1 minute.
7. Remove from heat; stir in yogurt.
8. Serve over fish.

Yield: 3 servings
Per Serving (1/2 cup):
  81 cal, 2 gm fat, 5 gm pro, 10 gm carb, 2 mg chol, 298 mg sodium, 0 gm dietary fiber

Lean Ways
with Beef,
Pork & Veal

Lean Ways with Beef, Pork & Veal

Lean Ways with Beef, Pork & Veal

Beef Broccoli Stir-Fry   Cindy Wachtler, R.D.

1 lb. lean top round
   steak, trimmed of fat
1 lg. bunch fresh broccoli
   (approx. 2 lb.)

1 tsp. peanut oil
1 tsp. minced garlic
2 T. water

SAUCE:
2 tsp. cornstarch
1 c. beef broth

1 tsp. light soy sauce
1/4 to 1/2 tsp. white or
   black pepper

MARINADE:
2 tsp. sake (rice wine)
   or sherry
1/2 tsp. baking soda
2 T. light soy sauce

1 1/2 tsp. cornstarch
1 tsp. peanut oil
1/2 tsp. sugar
1/2 tsp. ginger

1. Trim beef of all fat, then slice across the grain into 1/8-inch strips.
2. Combine marinade ingredients in medium bowl. Add beef strips and mix well; let stand 20 to 30 minutes to tenderize.
3. Trim tough stems and leaves from broccoli. Break tops into bite-size florets and cut stems into 1/2-inch slices.
4. Combine sauce ingredients in small bowl; set aside.
5. Heat a large nonstick skillet or wok until very hot. Add beef strips with marinade. Stir-fry over highest possible heat until lightly browned. Remove beef from skillet; set aside.
6. Heat 1 teaspoon peanut oil in the same skillet. Add garlic and prepared broccoli. Stir-fry over high heat for 3 to 5 minutes until broccoli is crisp-tender. Add 2 tablespoons water; cover tightly and steam over medium heat for 3 minutes.
7. Remove lid; add sauce ingredients. Stir until sauce bubbles. Add beef; heat through and serve immediately.

Yield: 4 servings
Per Serving:
266 cal, 10 gm fat, 32 gm pro, 16 gm carb, 70 mg chol, 723 mg sodium, 6 gm dietary fiber

Beef Burgundy

Patty Kirk, R.D.

1 lb. lean top round steak, sliced thinly into 1" strips
2 tsp. vegetable oil
2 c. onion, sliced
2 c. carrots, sliced
1/3 c. burgundy or any dry red wine
1 3/4 c. beef broth
1 (4 oz.) can sliced mushrooms, undrained
1 T. worcestershire sauce
2 T. cornstarch
1/4 c. water
Nonstick vegetable cooking spray

1. Spray skillet with cooking spray.
2. Sauté steak strips in oil until brown. Add onion; cook 2 minutes longer.
3. Stir in carrots, wine, broth, mushrooms with liquid and worcestershire sauce. Bring to a boil. Reduce heat; cover and simmer 20 minutes.
4. Dissolve cornstarch in the 1/4 cup water, then stir into meat mixture. Cook, stirring constantly until thickened.
5. Serve over bed of fluffy, hot rice. This dish is also great served over cooked noodles.

Yield: 4 servings
Per Serving:
   292 cal, 10 gm fat, 28 gm pro, 21 gm carb, 70 mg chol, 654 mg sodium, 4 gm dietary fiber

Beef Shishkabobs

Georgia Kostas, M.P.H., R.D.

1 lb. lean meat (filet, sirloin, chuck), cut into chunks & trimmed of fat
1/2 c. fat-free Italian dressing
1/2 c. red wine
8 cherry tomatoes
1/2 onion, cut into 8 chunks
1/2 green bell pepper, cut into 8 chunks
1 zucchini, cut into 8 chunks
4 skewers

1. Marinate meat overnight in salad dressing and wine, turning once.
2. On each skewer, alternate 1/4 of the meat chunks, 2 cherry tomatoes, 2 chunks of onion, 2 chunks of green bell pepper, and 2 chunks of zucchini.
3. On a charcoal grill or in an oven broiler, cook shishkabobs 10 to 15 minutes each side, turning as needed to cook evenly throughout.

Yield: 4 servings
Per Servings (1 shishkabob):
   222 cal, 10 gm fat, 24 gm pro, 6 gm carb, 73 mg chol, 161 mg sodium, 2 gm dietary fiber

Steak with Rice Dressing   Brenda Mack

1 1/2 lb. top round steak	1 (2 1/2 oz.) can mushrooms,
1/4 c. flour	chopped & drained
1/8 tsp. pepper	1 tsp. thyme
2 T. flour	1/8 tsp. pepper
4 beef bouillon cubes in	Nonstick vegetable
2 c. hot water	cooking spray
3 c. cooked brown rice or	
combination of brown &	
wild rice	

1. Tenderize meat by pounding it with a meat mallet; cut into 6 pieces.
2. Combine flour and pepper; pour on a plate and coat both sides of meat.
3. Spray a skillet with cooking spray; brown meat.
4. Remove meat from skillet; in same skillet add the 2 tablespoons flour and cook until lightly browned.
5. Mix beef bouillon cubes with hot water; add 1/4 cup to skillet and stir to combine.
6. Add 3/4 cup more broth. Mixture will be slightly lumpy. Use a whisk to remove some of the lumps.
7. Remove from heat and add cooked rice, mushrooms, thyme and pepper.
8. Place 1/2 of dressing mixture in 1 1/2- to 2-quart covered casserole dish; top with meat and then other half of dressing.
9. Pour second half of broth (1 cup) over casserole.
10. Cover and bake at 325°F. for 1 hour and 15 minutes, or microwave on full power for 15 to 20 minutes, until meat is tender.

Yield: 6 servings
Per Serving:
   320 cal, 8 gm fat, 28 gm pro, 33 gm carb, 70 mg chol, 782 mg sodium, 2 gm dietary fiber

Roast meats on a rack to allow the fat to drip off into the pan.

Oriental Shredded Beef and Vegetables

Cindy Kleckner, R.D.

6 oz. beef tenderloin or
  chicken breast
1/2 c. carrots, shredded
1/2 c. celery, thinly sliced
1/4 c. green onions,
  shredded
1/4 c. green bell pepper,
  shredded
1/2 T. oil

1 T. ginger, chopped; or
  1/4 to 1/2 tsp. ginger
  powder
1 T. light soy sauce
1/2 tsp. sugar
2 tsp. Tabasco sauce (or
  to desired taste)
1/2 tsp. vinegar
2 T. water
1 c. cooked rice

To Prepare:
1. Slice beef (or chicken) against grain into thin strips.
2. Chop, slice, dice vegetables as desired. (May use any variation you like i.e., broccoli, cauliflower, etc.)

To Cook:
1. Heat oil in wok or nonstick skillet; stir-fry beef (or chicken) until browned. Remove from wok or skillet.
2. Reserve oil and sauté all vegetables for 1 to 2 minutes. Remove.
3. Add ginger, soy sauce, sugar, Tabasco sauce, vinegar and water; heat until dissolved. Add beef (or chicken) and vegetables to the sauce and stir for 1 minute over high heat.
4. Serve over rice.

Yield: 2 servings
Per Serving:
314 cal, 10 gm fat, 20 gm pro, 36 gm carb, 49 mg chol, 465 mg sodium, 3 gm dietary fiber

*A large roast or turkey can be carved
easily after it stands for 30 minutes.*

Hobo Stew

Cindy Kleckner, R.D.

1 1/2 lb. round steak, cut
    into 1" cubes
1 (16 oz.) can tomatoes
1 (8 oz.) can tomato sauce
1 med. onion, sliced
1 tsp. worcestershire sauce
1/2 tsp. basil

1/4 tsp. rosemary
1/4 tsp. pepper
4 med. potatoes, cut into
    1/2" cubes
1 (10 oz.) pkg. frozen
    mixed vegetables

1. Combine all ingredients in a 3-quart casserole dish or crockpot.
2. Cook 3 to 4 hours; stir about 4 times during cooking.
3. If crockpot is used, put on low setting and cook for 8 to 10 hours.

Yield: 6 servings
Per Serving:
    290 cal, 7 gm fat, 29 gm pro, 28 gm carb, 70 mg chol, 437 mg sodium,
    6 gm dietary fiber

No Peek Beef Stew

Brenda Mack

6 potatoes, peeled & cut
    into lg. pieces
8 carrots, peeled & sliced
    thick
1 1/4 lb cubed lean stew
    meat
1 slice bread, cubed

1 c. celery, chopped
1 lg. onion, cut into
    quarters
1 T. tapioca
1 T. sugar
1 c. tomato juice
1 (2 1/2 lb.) can tomatoes

1. Combine all ingredients in large covered pan (2 1/2 to 5-quart Dutch oven).
2. Cook in preheated oven (250°F.) for 5 hours. Do not lift lid during cooking.

Yield: 12 servings
Per Serving:
    173 cal, 3 gm fat, 13 gm pro, 23 gm carb, 29 mg chol, 278 mg sodium,
    4 gm dietary fiber

Little Porcupine Balls

Pat McDonald

1 lb. lean ground round
1/2 c. uncooked rice
1 T. onion, finely chopped
2 T. green bell pepper,
    finely chopped
1 tsp. salt

1/2 tsp. celery flakes
Dash of garlic powder
2 c. tomato juice
1/2 tsp. cinnamon
2 T. sugar
1 T. worcestershire sauce

1. Combine uncooked rice, beef, onion, green bell pepper, salt, celery flakes and garlic powder.
2. Form into balls about 1 1/2-inches in diameter.
3. Heat tomato juice, cinnamon, sugar, worcestershire sauce in skillet.
4. Drop in meat balls; cover tightly.
5. Simmer 30 minutes.
6. May serve over rice.

Yield: 8 servings
Per Serving:
    175 cal, 7 gm fat, 12 gm pro, 16 gm carb, 36 mg chol, 532 mg sodium, 1 gm dietary fiber

To reduce fat intake from meats, consume only those which contain 3 grams of fat or less per 1 ounce...such as filets, tenderloin cuts, top round, top sirloin and round roast.

Meatloaf with Mushroom Sauce

Dr. Kenneth Cooper

1/2 lb. skinless ground
   turkey breast
1/2 lb. lean ground beef
1/4 c. bread crumbs
1 egg white or 1/8 c. egg
   substitute
1 tsp. parsley
Pepper, to taste
1 tsp. diet margarine
2 T. green onions, chopped

1 garlic clove, minced
3 c. fresh mushrooms,
   sliced
1/2 c. dry red cooking wine
1 tsp. cornstarch
1/2 c. low-sodium beef
   broth
1 (15 oz.) can low-sodium
   whole tomatoes, drained
   & chopped (optional)

1. Mix turkey, beef, bread crumbs, egg white, parsley and pepper to taste.
2. Shape into a loaf and put in a loaf pan. Bake 1 hour at 350°F.
3. While loaf is cooking, prepare sauce. In a large nonstick skillet over medium heat, heat diet margarine until bubbly.
4. Stir in green onion and garlic; sauté 2 minutes.
5. Add mushrooms; sauté until tender.
6. Stir in wine. Bring to a boil and cook 1 minute.
7. Dissolve cornstarch in beef broth. Stir into the mushroom mixture. Bring to a boil and cook, stirring constantly, until slightly thickened.
8. Season with pepper, to taste.
9. Add tomatoes, if using.
10. To serve, remove meatloaf from pan and place on platter. Pour mushroom sauce over meatloaf, or serve on the side.

Yield: 5 servings
Per Serving:
   198 cal, 7 gm fat, 21 gm pro, 7 gm carb, 59 mg chol, 103 mg sodium, 1 gm dietary fiber

To make a fluffy meat loaf, beat egg whites stiff,
and add them after all other ingredients have been mixed.

Mom's Meatloaf

Barbara Costello

1 lb. lean ground beef
1 onion, chopped
1 green bell pepper, chopped
1 c. seasoned bread crumbs
2 T. picante sauce
2 egg whites

1/4 tsp. salt
1/4 tsp. pepper
1/4 tsp. seasoned salt
1/4 tsp. garlic powder
1 T. parsley
1/4 c. tomato sauce

1. Combine all ingredients except tomato sauce and place in loaf pan.
2. Bake at 350°F. for 1 hour, adding the tomato sauce on top during the last 15 minutes.

Yield: 6 servings
Per Serving:
   235 cal, 11 gm fat, 18 gm pro, 15 gm carb, 50 mg chol, 399 mg sodium, 2 gm dietary fiber

Jerry's Meatloaf

Susan Hill

1 1/2 lb. ground round
1/3 c. onion, chopped
1/3 c. green bell pepper, chopped
1/2 c. carrots, grated
3 slices wholewheat bread, toasted & torn into small pieces

2 egg whites
1 T. Mrs. Dash seasoning
1/4 c. ketchup
1/8 c. barbecue sauce
1/4 c. picante sauce
1 T. mustard
1/4 c. skim milk

SAUCE ON TOP:
1/4 c. ketchup

1/8 c. barbecue sauce
1/4 c. picante sauce

1. Mix all meatloaf ingredients together.
2. Shape meat into 1 loaf and place in shallow baking dish or use a meatloaf pan.
3. Bake in preheated 325°F. oven for 1 to 1 1/2 hours.
4. Mix together sauce ingredients; add sauce topping to meatloaf 15 minutes before baking is finished.

Yield: 1 large meatloaf (8 servings)
Per Serving:
   233 cal, 11 gm fat, 19 gm pro, 14 gm carb, 53 mg chol, 433 mg sodium, 2 gm dietary fiber

Tomato Chili

Veronica Coronado

8 oz. skinless ground
   turkey breast
8 oz. lean ground beef
1 1/2 tsp. minced garlic
1 onion, diced
3 (15 oz.) cans red kidney
   beans, rinsed & drained

1 (26 oz.) jar spaghetti
   sauce
1 (8 oz.) can tomato paste
3/4 c. water
4 T. chili powder

1. Brown meat, onion and garlic until meat is brown; drain fat well from meat.
2. Add other ingredients; simmer for 1 hour.

Yield: 10 servings
Per Serving:
   255 cal, 7 gm fat, 19 gm pro, 32 gm carb, 27 mg chol, 574 mg sodium, 7 gm dietary fiber

Typically, ground turkey includes light and dark meat with some skin added, so the fat content is high. To select lean ground turkey, purchase turkey breast and ask the butcher to remove skin and grind.

Mousaka

Georgia Kostas, M.P.H., R.D.

MEAT SAUCE:
1/2 lb. extra-lean ground
   beef
1 c. onion, chopped
1/2 tsp. minced garlic

1 tsp. salt
1/2 tsp. pepper
1/8 tsp. cinnamon
2 T. parsley
1 (8 oz.) can tomato sauce

EGGPLANT:
2 (1 1/4 lb.) med. eggplant
Nonstick vegetable
   cooking spray

1 tsp. sugar
1/4 tsp. cinnamon

CREAM SAUCE:
2 c. evaporated skimmed milk
2 T. flour

4 oz. low-fat cottage cheese
2 eggs or 1/2 c. egg
   substitute

TOPPING: 1/2 c. Romano cheese

Meat Sauce:
1. Brown beef in skillet. Drain off fat.
2. Add onion, garlic, salt, pepper, 1/8 teaspoon cinnamon, parsley and tomato sauce. Stir to combine and simmer 10 minutes.

Eggplant:
1. Wash eggplant. Slice into rounds (1/4-inch thick) and cut rounds in half.
2. Place on baking sheet; then spray both sides of eggplant with cooking spray.
3. Combine sugar and 1/4 teaspoon cinnamon. Sprinkle on eggplant.
4. Broil eggplant on each side for 3 minutes.
5. Using a 9x13-inch baking pan, layer eggplant slices alternately with meat mixture, topping with eggplant.

Cream Sauce:
1. Heat milk in saucepan.
2. Add flour, stirring in slowly with a whisk. Stir in cottage cheese.
3. Slowly add slightly beaten eggs and cook over low heat until mixture thickens, stirring regularly with whisk.
4. Pour over eggplant/ meat mixture and top with Romano cheese.
5. Bake, covered, at 350°F. for 30 minutes. May cook 5 minutes more without cover to brown the top.

Yield: 9 servings
Per Serving:
   182 cal, 6 gm fat, 15 gm pro, 17 gm carb, 70 mg chol, 624 mg sodium, 2 gm dietary fiber

Marinated Pork Tenderloin

Patty Kirk, R.D.

2 lb. pork tenderloin
1/2 tsp. ginger
1/2 med. onion, minced
2 cloves garlic, minced

2 tsp. basil
1 1/2 tsp. parsley
3 T. light soy sauce
1 T. vegetable oil

1. Combine all ingredients except tenderloin; process in food processor or blender until well mixed.
2. Pour over pork tenderloin; marinate for 1 hour or overnight.
3. Grill over hot coals or gas grill, low to medium heat, or bake in oven at 350° for 30 to 45 minutes. Use a meat thermometer in thickest part of the meat. Doneness is indicated when temperature reaches 170°F.

Yield: 8 servings
Per Serving:
148 cal, 5 gm fat, 25 gm pro, 1 gm carb, 79 mg chol, 23 mg sodium, 0 gm dietary fiber

Veal Scaloppine

Patty Kirk, R.D.

8 oz. (2 c.) fresh mush-
   rooms, sliced
1/8 tsp. pepper
1/2 c. dry white wine
16 oz. (four 4 oz. pieces)
   veal scaloppine

2 T. flour
2 tsp. olive oil
3/4 c. onion, very finely
   chopped
1 c. chicken broth

1. Place mushrooms, pepper and wine in a small saucepan; simmer, uncovered, for about 10 minutes until mushrooms are tender.
2. Pound the veal with flat side of meat mallet or with a rolling pin to half the original thickness. Dredge with flour.
3. Heat olive oil in a large nonstick skillet over high heat. Add onion and shake pan to distribute onion evenly.
4. Arrange breaded cutlets on bed of onion in skillet; cook for 1 to 2 minutes over high heat until meat begins to brown. Turn and cook 1 to 2 minutes to brown other side.
5. Reduce heat to low, add broth, and simmer for 2 minutes.
6. Turn veal and add the mushroom mixture. Increase the heat; cook for 3 to 5 minutes until fluid is reduced and sauce is slightly thickened.

Yield: 4 servings
Per Serving:
216 cal, 6 gm fat, 27 gm pro, 17 gm carb, 88 mg chol, 256 mg sodium, 1 gm dietary fiber

Orange Sauce for Pork or Poultry

Brenda Mack

2 oranges	1 T. cornstarch
1 T. sugar	1 c. orange juice

1. Peel and section oranges; cut sections into 1/2-inch pieces and set aside.
2. Combine sugar and cornstarch; stir in 1 cup orange juice.
3. Cook and stir over medium heat until thickened and bubbly.
4. Add orange pieces
5. Cook and stir 1 to 2 minutes more.
6. Serve warm sauce over cooked pork tenderloin or skinless chicken breasts.

Yield: 6 servings
Per Serving:
  53 cal, 0 gm fat, 1 gm pro, 13 gm carb, 0 mg chol, 0 mg sodium, 1 gm dietary fiber

Red Wine and Mushroom Sauce

Cindy Kleckner, R.D.

1 tsp. diet margarine	1/2 c. red cooking wine
2 T. green onions, minced	1 tsp. cornstarch
1/2 tsp. minced garlic	1/2 c. low-sodium beef
3 c. fresh mushrooms, sliced	broth
	Freshly ground pepper

1. In a large nonstick skillet over medium heat, heat margarine until bubbly; stir in green onions and garlic.
2. Sauté 2 minutes; DO NOT BROWN.
3. Add mushrooms; sauté until tender.
4. Stir in wine; bring to a boil and cook 1 minute.
5. Dissolve cornstarch in beef broth; stir into mushroom mixture and bring to a boil.
6. Cook 1 minute, stirring constantly.
7. Season to taste with pepper; serve with poultry, fish or veal.

Yield: 2 servings
Per Serving (1 cup):
  92 cal, 1 gm fat, 3 gm pro, 8 gm carb, 0 mg chol, 36 mg sodium, 1 gm dietary fiber

Meatless
Meals

Meatless Meals

Meatless Meals

Vegetarian Black Bean Chili

Nutrition Staff

1 (24 oz.) pkg. dried black
  beans
1 T. cumin seeds
1 1/2 tsp. oregano
1 1/2 tsp. basil
2 1/2 T. diet margarine
3/4 c. onion, diced
3/4 c. green bell pepper,
  finely chopped
1 1/2 c. carrots, sliced

1 tsp. minced garlic
2 tsp. paprika
1/2 tsp. ground red pepper
1/4 tsp. salt (optional)
1 1/2 c. canned tomatoes,
  low-sodium, crushed
1 to 2 fresh or pickled
  jalapeño peppers, seeds
  removed & minced

TOPPING:
5 oz. low-fat Cheddar
  cheese, grated

10 T. plain nonfat yogurt

1. Cook beans according to package directions or soak overnight in 7 cups of water and cook on low in crockpot 8 to 10 hours.
2. Remove 1/2 cup liquid from beans and reserve.
3. Drain beans and combine with reserved 1/2 cup liquid; set aside.
4. In a small nonstick skillet over medium-low heat, toast cumin seeds, oregano and basil, shaking pan occasionally for 3 minutes until fragrant; set aside.
5. In a large pan over medium-high heat, heat margarine until bubbly; add onion, green pepper, carrots, garlic, paprika, red pepper and salt.
6. Sauté 10 minutes, stirring frequently until onion is soft.
7. Add tomatoes, jalapeño pepper and toasted cumin seed mixture; bring to a boil.
8. Add beans and liquid; continue to simmer, stirring frequently until chili is heated thoroughly.
9. To serve, place 1/2 ounce cheese (2 tablespoons) in each bowl. Top with 1 cup chili mixture and 1 tablespoon yogurt.

Yield: 10 servings
Per Serving (1 cup):
  322 cal, 5 gm fat, 21 gm pro, 50 gm carb, 8 mg chol, 169 mg sodium, 5 gm dietary fiber

Cuban Black Beans and Brown Rice

Barbara Bartolomeo

1 lb. dried black beans
3 qt. water
1 onion, cut into squares
1 tsp. minced garlic
2 T. olive oil
1 green bell pepper, seeds removed & cut into 8 pieces
1 can non-alcoholic beer
2 T. vinegar
1 tsp. salt
2 T. sugar
4 c. cooked brown rice
Green onions, minced (optional)
Plain nonfat yogurt (optional)
Picante sauce (optional)

1. Soak beans in water overnight in crockpot.
2. In the morning, drain beans and add enough water to cover beans 1-inch. Set crockpot on medium.
3. Add olive oil, beer, onion, green pepper, salt and sugar; mix well.
4. Cook until done, about 6 to 8 hours.
5. Serve over brown rice.
6 . Garnish with minced green onions, yogurt and picante sauce.

Yield: 8 servings
Per Serving:
375 cal, 5 gm fat, 15 gm pro, 69 gm carb, 0 mg chol, 271 mg sodium, 6 gm dietary fiber

For a ready supply of bread crumbs, save the heels from all your bread plus any stale bread. Place in a plastic bag and freeze until needed. Make crumbs by putting the frozen slices in a blender or food processor. You can also make crumbs first, then freeze for use in any recipe calling for fresh crumbs.

Cajun-Style Red Beans and Brown Rice

Cindy Kleckner, R.D.

1 lb. dried pinto beans
2 c. yellow onion, chopped
1 c. green onions, chopped
1 c. green bell pepper, chopped
1/2 tsp. minced garlic
1/4 tsp. red cayenne pepper
3/4 tsp. pepper
1/2 tsp. salt

1/4 tsp. oregano
1/4 tsp. garlic powder
1 T. worcestershire sauce
3 dashes Tabasco sauce
6 oz. tomato paste
1/4 tsp. thyme
1 tsp. celery flakes
6 c. cooked brown rice

1. Wash beans and then soak for 12 hours.
2. Drain water.
3. Fill a large pot with beans; add water to 1/2-inch above beans.
4. Add remaining ingredients; cook over low heat 2 to 2 1/2 hours, covered.
5. Serve over cooked brown rice.

Yield: 9 servings
Per Servings (1 cup beans, 2/3 cup rice):
   368 cal, 2 gm fat, 16 gm pro, 75 gm carb, 0 mg chol, 167 mg sodium, 14 gm dietary fiber

*Citrus fruit yields nearly twice the amount of
juice if it is dropped into hot water a few minutes
or rolled beneath your hand before squeezing.*

Potatoes Stuffed with Vegetarian Chili

Cindy Wachtler, R.D.

8 med. baking potatoes
1/4 lb. fresh mushrooms,
 sliced
1/2 c. onion, chopped
1/3 c. green bell pepper,
 chopped
1/2 tsp. minced garlic
1 (16 oz.) can red kidney
 beans, undrained
1 (14 oz.) can stewed
 tomatoes, undrained

1/4 tsp. cumin
1/8 tsp. hot sauce
1/8 tsp. red pepper
1/8 tsp. whole oregano
1/2 c. (2 oz.) Monterey
 Jack cheese, shredded
3 T. green onions, sliced,
 for garnish
Nonstick vegetable
 cooking spray

1. Prick potatoes with a fork; bake at 400°F. for 1 hour, or until tender. Wrap in aluminum foil and keep warm.
2. Coat a large saucepan with cooking spray; place over medium heat until hot. Add mushrooms, onion, green pepper and garlic; sauté 5 minutes or until tender.
3. Stir in next 6 ingredients; cook over low heat just until thoroughly heated, stirring occasionally.
4. Remove foil from potatoes. Split tops lengthwise and fluff pulp with a fork. Arrange in a 13x9x2-inch baking dish. Spoon chili mixture evenly over potatoes; top with cheese.
5. Bake at 400°F. for 5 to 7 minutes or until cheese melts. Garnish with green onions.

Yield: 8 servings
Per Serving (1 potato with chili):
 344 cal, 3 gm fat, 11 gm pro, 71 gm carb, 7 mg chol, 333 mg sodium, 14 gm dietary fiber

A 5-ounce cup of brewed tea contains 40 mg caffeine.

Herbed Lentils and Rice

Georgia Kostas, M.P.H., R.D.

2 2/3 c. chicken broth
3/4 c. dried lentils
3/4 c. green onions, chopped
1/2 c. brown rice, uncooked
1/4 c. wine
1/2 tsp. basil

1/8 tsp. salt
1/4 tsp. oregano
1/4 tsp. thyme
1/8 tsp. garlic powder
1/2 c. (2 oz.) low-fat Swiss
  cheese, grated

1. Preheat oven to 350°.
2. Combine all ingredients except cheese in casserole dish.
3. Bake, covered, for 1 1/2 to 2 hours, stirring twice.
4. Remove from oven; top immediately with grated cheese and serve.

Yield: 6 servings
Per Serving:
   191 cal, 3 gm fat, 13 gm pro, 27 gm carb, 6 mg chol, 444 mg sodium,
   5 gm dietary fiber

Fried Rice

Veronica Coronado

1 T. vegetable oil
2 c. cooked brown rice,
  prepared the day before
2 1/2 tsp. light soy sauce
2 green onions, sliced

1/2 c. egg substitute
4 to 6 T. cooked chicken or
  shrimp, minced (optional)
1/4 c. frozen peas
1/8 tsp. white pepper

1. Heat oil in skillet; add rice.
2. Stir-fry until rice is hot and mixed with oil.
3. Add soy sauce; mix well.
4. If rice is dry, add 1 to 2 tablespoons water; cover and cook gently until
   water is absorbed.
5. Stir in green onion.
6. Push rice to side of skillet.
7. Pour egg substitute into center of rice mixture and quickly scramble
   with a fork.
8. As egg sets, stir gently to let uncooked egg flow underneath.
9. Stir cooked egg into rice, breaking egg into small pieces.
10. Stir in peas, white pepper and meat; heat through.

Yield: 2 servings
Per Serving (1 1/2 cups):
   347 cal, 8 gm fat, 12 gm pro, 57 gm carb, 0 mg chol, 351 mg sodium,
   5 gm dietary fiber

Open-Faced Swiss and Pear Sandwiches

Cindy Kleckner, R.D.

4 slices wholewheat bread
4 (1 oz.) slices low-fat
   Swiss cheese

2 med. pears, pared, cored
   & sliced
1/2 tsp. cinnamon

1. Preheat oven on broil.
2. Toast bread; place a cheese slice on each piece of toast.
3. Arrange sliced pears on cheese; sprinkle cinnamon on pears.
4. Broil 10 minutes or until lightly browned.
5. Serve hot.

Yield: 4 servings
Per Serving (1 sandwich):
   197 cal, 6 gm fat, 11 gm pro, 26 gm carb, 15 mg chol, 283 mg sodium,
   4 gm dietary fiber

Cheesy Pita Pocket Sandwich

Cindy Kleckner, R.D.

1 wholewheat pita pocket
1 oz. part-skim mozzarella
   cheese, grated
1 T. tomato, chopped

Lettuce, shredded
1 T. green onions, chopped
1 tsp. Italian dressing

1. Cut pita bread in half crosswise.
2. Fill each half with mozzarella cheese.
3. Top the cheese with tomato, lettuce and green onions.
4. Pour Italian dressing into each half and serve.

Yield: 1 serving
Per Serving (1 sandwich):
   274 cal, 8 gm fat, 14 gm pro, 36 gm carb, 15 mg chol, 532 mg sodium,
   4 gm dietary fiber

Try these additional delicious meatless meals in our cookbook

Working Woman's Lasagna

Artichoke-Stuffed Manicotti

Spinach Manicotti

Fettuccine Alfredo

Eggplant Parmesan

Stuffed Shells

Garlic Spaghetti with Chili Pepper

Angel Hair Pasta with Tomato Basil Sauce

Alexandra's Favorite Pasta

Colorful Pasta Dinner

Ricotta-Parmesan Torte

Spicy Bean Enchiladas

Tostadas

Continued on following page.

Continued from preceding page.

Mexican Bean Bake

Pizza Olé

Mexican Pizza Stacks

Mama Mía

Mama Mía

Mama Mía

Zucchini Lasagna

Brenda Mack

5 zucchini (1 1/2 lb.)
1/2 lb. extra-lean ground
    beef
1 (8 oz.) can tomato sauce
1/2 tsp. basil
1/2 tsp. oregano
1/4 tsp. salt

1/8 tsp. garlic powder
1 c. low-fat cottage cheese
1/4 c. egg substitute or
    2 egg whites
1/4 c. dry bread crumbs
3/4 c. part-skim mozzarella
    cheese, shredded

1. Slice unpeeled zucchini lengthwise to make lasagna noodle-like strips.
2. Cook zucchini in water until translucent and tender. Drain.
3. Cook ground beef. Drain and return to skillet.
4. Add tomato sauce, basil, oregano, salt and garlic powder to beef. Simmer for 5 minutes.
5. Combine cottage cheese and egg substitute in a small bowl.
6. In an 8-inch square baking pan layer 1/2 of each: zucchini (to cover bottom of pan), bread crumbs, meat mixture, cottage cheese mixture and mozzarella cheese. Repeat with other 1/2 of ingredients. Cover with foil.
7. Bake in preheated oven (350°F.) for 30 minutes until heated through. If too soupy, bake uncovered for a few more minutes.

Optional: May add layers of mushrooms.

Yield: 6 servings
Per Serving:
188 cal, 8 gm fat, 18 gm pro, 12 gm carb, 35 mg chol, 609 mg sodium, 1 gm dietary fiber

To save time, double or triple a recipe and freeze the extras.

Working Woman's Lasagna

Mary Ellen England, R.D.

1 (28 oz.) jar spaghetti
    sauce
1 c. water
16 oz. low-fat cottage
    cheese
1/4 c. egg substitute
8 oz. (2 c.) part-skim
    mozzarella cheese,
    grated
1 tsp. garlic powder

1/4 tsp. pepper
1 (8 oz.) pkg. lasagna
    noodles, uncooked
1 (10 oz.) box frozen
    spinach, cooked &
    drained; or 10 oz.
    sliced zucchini
Nonstick vegetable
    cooking spray

1. Preheat oven to 375°F.
2. Spray bottom of casserole dish with cooking spray.
3. Add water to sauce.
4. Mix cottage cheese and egg substitute with seasoning and 1/4 cup of mozzarella cheese.
5. Lightly cover the bottom of casserole dish with sauce.
6. Place a layer of _raw_ noodles on bottom of casserole dish.
7. Cover noodles with sauce.
8. Drop spoonfuls of cheese mixture over sauce.
9. Layer vegetables.
10. Layer noodles, sauce, cheese mixture and remaining sauce. Be sure to cover noodles well with sauce.
11. Bake, uncovered, 40 to 50 minutes.
12. Sprinkle remaining mozzarella cheese over lasagna during last 15 minutes of baking.

Yield: 8 servings
Per Serving:
    300 cal, 10 gm fat, 22 gm pro, 33 gm carb, 47 mg chol, 820 mg sodium, 3 gm dietary fiber

Parsley will keep a long time in the refrigerator if, after washing it, you place it in a covered jar while still slightly damp.

Artichoke-Stuffed Manicotti

Pam Peterson

8 manicotti shells
2 tsp. olive oil
3/4 c. red onion, chopped
1 1/2 c. frozen artichoke
    hearts, thawed & chop-
    ped; or canned artichoke
    hearts, chopped
3 tsp. parsley
3/4 tsp. thyme
1/4 tsp. salt

1/2 c. chicken broth
1/2 c. part-skim ricotta
    cheese
2 tsp. Parmesan cheese
3/4 c. spaghetti sauce with
    mushrooms
2 oz. part-skim mozzarella
    cheese, shredded
Nonstick vegetable
    cooking spray

1. In a large pot of boiling water, cook manicotti shells 6 minutes (slightly firm); drain.
2. In a large nonstick skillet, heat olive oil on medium heat; add onion and sauté 2 to 3 minutes, or until tender.
3. Add chopped artichoke hearts, 2 teaspoons parsley, thyme and salt; sauté 2 minutes.
4. Add chicken broth to skillet; cook, stirring frequently 6 to 7 minutes until liquid evaporates.
5. Remove skillet from heat; stir in ricotta and Parmesan cheeses.
6. Spread 1/4 cup spaghetti sauce in bottom of baking dish sprayed with cooking spray.
7. Spoon artichoke filling into manicotti shells; place in baking dish.
8. Add rest of spaghetti sauce on top of manicotti; cover with foil and bake at 350°F. for 20 minutes. Remove foil.
9. Sprinkle mozzarella cheese and remaining parsley over shells; bake another 10 to 12 minutes, or until cheese melts and filling is hot.

Yield: 4 servings
Per Serving (2 manicotti):
    287 cal, 10 gm fat, 15 gm pro, 37 gm carb, 18 mg chol, 560 mg sodium, 3 gm dietary fiber

*Fresh tomatoes keep longer if stored in
the refrigerator with stems down.*

Spinach Manicotti

Susan Hoobler

1 (26 oz.) jar spaghetti
   sauce
1 (8 oz.) pkg. manicotti
   noodles
1 c. part-skim ricotta cheese
1 c. low-fat cottage cheese

2 1/2 oz. fresh spinach,
   torn into small pieces
1 1/2 c. part-skim mozza-
   rella cheese, grated
1/4 tsp. garlic powder

1. Combine ricotta cheese, cottage cheese, spinach, 3/4 cup mozzarella cheese and garlic powder.
2. Stuff uncooked noodles with cheese mixture.
3. Pour 1/3 of spaghetti sauce in 13x9x2-inch pan; place stuffed noodles in pan and cover with rest of spaghetti sauce.
4. Fill sauce jar halfway with water, shake and pour over noodles, making sure noodles are completely covered. Cover with foil.
5. Bake at 350°F. for 45 to 50 minutes.
6. Remove from oven; sprinkle remaining cheese over noodles and bake uncovered until cheese is melted, about 5 to 10 minutes.

Yield: 7 servings
Per Serving (2 manicotti):
   318 cal, 11 gm fat, 20 gm pro, 36 gm carb, 26 mg chol, 726 mg sodium, 3 gm dietary fiber

Before using the pulp of citrus fruits, grate the peel, being careful not to include the bitter-tasting inner white rind. Place in a tightly covered container and freeze until needed.

Fettuccine Alfredo
Jean Wisner, R.D.

8 oz. fettuccine, uncooked
Nonstick vegetable cooking
   spray
3/4 c. evaporated skimmed
   milk
1/3 c. (1 1/2 oz.) freshly
   grated Parmesan cheese
1 T. onion, minced
1 T. fresh chives, snipped

1 T. fresh basil, snipped
1 T. fresh parsley, snipped
1/4 tsp. lemon peel, finely
   shredded
1/4 tsp. garlic powder
1/8 tsp. pepper
Fresh basil sprig & lemon
   slices for garnish (optional)

1. Cook pasta according to package directions.
2. Drain; immediately spray with cooking spray. Place in a glass dish.
3. Add evaporated skimmed milk, Parmesan cheese, onion, chives, basil, parsley, lemon peel, garlic powder and pepper.
4. Cook in microwave, uncovered, on medium-high heat 6 to 10 minutes.
5. Toss lightly; garnish with basil and lemon slices.

Yield: 6 servings
Per Serving:
   205 cal, 4 gm fat, 11 gm pro, 32 gm carb, 7 mg chol, 179 mg sodium, 1 gm dietary fiber

Eggplant Parmesan
Jean Wisner, R.D.

3/4 c. Italian bread crumbs
2 egg whites plus 2 T. water
1 lg. eggplant, peeled &
   sliced 1/2" thick
3 c. spaghetti sauce

1/2 c. part-skim mozzarella
   cheese
3/4 c. Parmesan cheese
Nonstick vegetable
   cooking spray

1. Dip eggplant slices in egg white, then into bread crumbs.
2. Coat a large 12x18-inch baking sheet with cooking spray. Place eggplant slices on baking sheet and coat with cooking spray.
3. Bake at 375°F. for 30 minutes and remove from oven.
4. Pour 1/2 cup spaghetti sauce in a 9x13-inch Pyrex dish. Layer eggplant slices, sauce and mozzarella cheese. Top with Parmesan cheese.
5. Bake at 375°F. for 30 minutes.

Yield: 9 servings
Per Serving:
   136 cal, 6 gm fat, 8 gm protein, 14 gm carb, 9 mg chol, 518 mg sodium, 2 gm dietary fiber

Stuffed Shells

Nutrition Staff

3/4 of a 12 oz. pkg. large
   shells (21 shells)
1 (10 oz.) box frozen chopped spinach, thawed &
   drained
1 onion, chopped
2 tsp. diet margarine
2 egg whites, beaten

2/3 c. part-skim ricotta
   cheese
1/2 c. Parmesan cheese
1/2 tsp. nutmeg
1 recipe Original Tomato
   Sauce (See Index); or
   1 (28 oz.) jar meatless
   spaghetti sauce

1. Cook shells according to directions on package.
2. Defrost and squeeze excess water from spinach.
3. In skillet, cook onion in margarine until tender.
4. Add spinach; heat through.
5. Combine eggs, ricotta cheese, Parmesan cheese, nutmeg and spinach mixture.
6. Pour half the Original Tomato Sauce in a baking dish.
7. Stuff shells with filling; arrange in dish and top with remaining sauce.
8. Cover with aluminum foil and bake in a 350°F. preheated oven for 30
   minutes.

Yield: 7 servings
Per Serving (3 shells):
   282 cal, 7 gm fat, 14 gm pro, 42 gm carb, 12 mg chol, 293 mg sodium,
   6 gm dietary fiber

*Utilize low-fat commercial tomato
sauces to make a quick pasta meal.
Also, try boil-in-bag rice, topped with
shrimp and sauce for a quick creole dish.*

Baked Spaghetti

Brenda Mack

3/4 lb. extra-lean ground
   beef
1/3 c. onion, chopped
1 clove garlic, minced
1/2 tsp. oregano
1/2 tsp. salt
1/4 tsp. pepper
1 (4 oz.) can sliced mushrooms (do not drain)

1 (16 oz.) jar meatless
   spaghetti sauce
8 oz. spaghetti, cooked
   & drained
1/3 c. light sour cream
1 c. low-fat cottage cheese
1/4 c. Parmesan cheese
Nonstick vegetable
   cooking spray

1. Sauté ground beef, onion, garlic, oregano, salt and pepper in a large skillet until meat is browned; pour off fat.
2. Stir in undrained mushrooms and spaghetti sauce; simmer uncovered for 10 minutes.
3. Place half the cooked spaghetti in bottom of a deep 8-inch square casserole dish that has been sprayed with cooking spray.
4. Layer half the meat mixture on top of spaghetti.
5. Combine the sour cream and cottage cheese; spread over meat mixture layer.
6. Add remaining spaghetti and cover with remaining meat mixture.
7. Sprinkle with Parmesan cheese.
8. Cover with foil and bake at 375°F. for 35 minutes; let stand for 5 minutes. Cut in squares and serve.

Yield: 8 servings
Per Serving:
   267 cal, 9 gm fat, 18 gm pro, 28 gm carb, 32 mg chol, 624 mg sodium, 2 gm dietary fiber

One gram of carbohydrate equals 4 calories.

Garlic Spaghetti with Chili Pepper

Cindy Kleckner, R.D.

1 lb. spaghetti	5 cloves garlic
2 T. olive oil	1/2 tsp. chili pepper

1. Cook the pasta following the directions on the package.
2. Meanwhile, heat olive oil and add garlic. (This is either left whole and removed before serving or it is finely chopped and not removed.)
3. Add the chili pepper; cook until the garlic is golden brown.
4. The moment the pasta is ready, drain it and put into a large serving bowl.
5. Pour the sizzling oil over the pasta, stirring well.
6. Serve immediately.

Yield: 8 servings
Per serving:
231 cal, 4 gm fat, 7 gm pro, 40 gm carb, 0 mg chol, 21 mg sodium, 1 gm dietary fiber

Easy Vegetable Linguine

Harriet Guthrie

2 oz. Canadian bacon, cut into small pieces	3 oz. linguine, cooked & drained
1 c. broccoli florets	1/2 c. cherry tomato halves
1/4 c. onion, chopped	1/4 c. Parmesan cheese
1 1/2 tsp. olive oil	

1. Sauté Canadian bacon, broccoli and onion in olive oil.
2. Combine with cooked linguine, Parmesan cheese and tomatoes; mix lightly.
3. Serve warm.

Yield: 2 servings
Per serving:
312 cal, 10 gm fat, 19 gm pro, 38 gm carb, 24 mg chol, 640 mg sodium, 4 gm dietary fiber

Angel Hair Pasta with Tomato Basil Sauce

Susan Smith

2 T. olive oil
1 1/2 tsp. minced garlic
1/4 c. green onions, sliced
3 lg. tomatoes or 9 roma
   tomatoes, peeled &
   diced
2 T. fresh basil, chopped;
   or 1/2 T. dry basil

3/4 tsp. salt
1/4 tsp. pepper
8 oz. angel hair pasta,
   uncooked
2 T. grated Parmesan
   cheese

1. In a large skillet, heat oil. Add garlic and green onions; stir-fry for 1 minute.
2. Stir in tomatoes, basil, salt and pepper; cook 2 minutes, stirring frequently.
3. Cook pasta according to package directions; drain.
4. Toss tomato mixture with hot cooked pasta. Sprinkle each serving with 1/2 tablespoon Parmesan cheese. Serve immediately.

Yield: 4 servings
Per Serving:
   298 cal, 9 gm fat, 9 gm pro, 46 gm carb, 2 mg chol, 461 mg sodium, 3 gm dietary fiber

One cup herbs on a paper towel in the microwave will dry in about 4 minutes. Crush and store in airtight container.

Shrimp and Blue Cheese Bow Tie Pasta

Veronica Coronado

1 1/2 qt. water
1 lb. med. fresh shrimp,
  unpeeled
3 c. broccoli florets
3 1/2 c. bow tie pasta
  (farfalle), uncooked
1 tsp. minced garlic

1/2 c. onion, chopped
2 tsp. olive oil
1 green bell pepper, cut
  into thin strips
1/2 c. blue cheese,
  coarsely crumbled
1/8 tsp. pepper

1. Bring water to a boil in a large pot; add shrimp, and cook 5 minutes.
2. Drain well; rinse with cold water.
3. Peel and devein shrimp; set aside.
4. Arrange broccoli in a vegetable steamer over boiling water.
5. Cover and steam 2 minutes; set aside.
6. Cook pasta according to package directions; drain well and set aside.
7. Sauté garlic and onion in oil in a large skillet over medium heat 1 minute; add bell pepper and sauté 2 minutes.
8. Remove from heat; add shrimp, broccoli, pasta and remaining ingredients, tossing gently.
9. Serve warm.

Yield: 4 servings
Per Serving:
  337 cal, 10 gm fat, 25 gm pro, 42 gm carb, 126 mg chol, 346 mg sodium, 6 gm dietary fiber

*Dry fresh bread when you need croutons or
crumbs in the microwave. One quart of cubes in
a rectangular dish will dry in 6 to 7 minutes. Stir a few times.*

Chicken Bow Tie Pasta   Veronica Coronado

1/4 c. sun-dried tomato
   bits (without salt or oil)
1/2 c. hot water
1 1/4 tsp. basil
1/4 tsp. salt
1/4 tsp. garlic powder
3 T. white wine vinegar
2 tsp. olive oil
1/8 tsp. Tabasco sauce

2 1/2 c. bow tie pasta
   (farfalle)
Nonstick vegetable
   cooking spray
1 lb. chicken breast, cut
   into small pieces
1 green bell pepper, chopped into small pieces
1 T. Parmesan cheese

1. Combine tomato bits and water in a bowl; cover and let stand 10 minutes. Drain.
2. Add basil and next 5 ingredients; stir well and set aside.
3. Cook pasta according to package directions; set aside.
4. Coat a large nonstick skillet with cooking spray; place over medium-high heat until hot; add chicken and sauté 5 minutes or until lightly browned.
5. Add bell pepper; sauté an additional 5 minutes or until chicken is done.
6. Combine chicken mixture, pasta and tomato mixture in a large bowl; toss gently.
7. Serve warm with Parmesan cheese lightly sprinkled on each serving.

Yield: 4 servings
Per Serving:
   305 cal, 7 gm fat, 32 gm pro, 27 gm carb, 97 mg chol, 234 mg sodium, 2 gm dietary fiber

To save time, buy food already prepared - shredded cheese, sliced turkey, pre-cooked and cubed chicken, chopped onions, minced garlic and pre-chopped vegetables.

Alexandra's Favorite Pasta

John R. Baer

2 tsp. olive oil
1 (28 oz.) can plum
   tomatoes, undrained
2 cloves garlic, minced
16 oz. spaghetti or
   fettuccine, uncooked

7 oz. part-skim mozzarella
   cheese, cut into 1/2"
   cubes
1/4 c. Parmesan cheese
1/8 tsp. red pepper flakes

1. Cube tomatoes; heat with juice over medium heat with garlic and olive oil for 20 minutes.
2. Meanwhile, cook pasta al dente, drain and place in serving bowl.
3. Add tomatoes, cheeses and red pepper flakes; toss.
4. Cover bowl for 5 minutes to allow cheeses to melt.
5. Toss again before serving.

Yield: 6 servings
Per Serving:
   415 cal, 10 gm fat, 21 gm pro, 60 gm carb, 20 mg chol, 461 mg sodium, 3 gm dietary fiber

Dietary fiber, or "roughage" consists of plant material that resists breakdown in the human digestive tract, causing food to pass through the colon more quickly, which prevents constipation.

Colorful Pasta Dinner

Georgia Kostas, M.P.H., R.D.

4 oz. rotini noodles, dry
2 carrots, cut in "coins"
2 c. broccoli florets, chopped
3 tsp. olive oil
1 tsp. minced garlic
1 onion, chopped
1/4 green bell pepper, chopped

1/4 yellow bell pepper, chopped
1/4 red bell pepper, chopped
2 T. pine nuts (optional)
3 T. fresh parsley, finely chopped
4 T. Parmesan cheese

1. Prepare pasta according to directions on package.
2. Steam carrots and broccoli in separate containers in microwave for 3 to 5 minutes (vegetables should be firm).
3. Sauté in skillet: oil, garlic, onion and all vegetables. Cook 5 minutes or until vegetables are tender.
4. Add cooked pasta and pine nuts; heat 1 minute.
5. Add parsley; toss.
6. Top with Parmesan cheese. Serve.

Yield: 4 servings
Per Serving:
202 cal, 6 gm fat, 9 gm pro, 31 gm carb, 4 mg chol, 115 mg sodium, 5 gm dietary fiber

Trim excess fat from meats before cooking.

Ricotta-Parmesan Torte

Nutrition Staff

DOUGH:
3/4 c. flour
3 T. warm water

1 T. plus 1 tsp. vegetable
oil
1/8 tsp. salt

FILLING:
1 T. margarine
1 c. green onions, minced
1 c. zucchini, grated
1/2 c. carrots, grated
2 cloves garlic, minced
2 c. cooked rice
1 c. part-skim ricotta
cheese

8 egg whites
3 T. Parmesan cheese,
divided
1/8 tsp. salt
1/8 tsp. freshly ground
pepper

To Prepare Dough:
1. In a small mixing bowl, combine flour, water, oil and salt.
2. Using your hands, knead dough into a smooth ball (dough should hold together but not be sticky; if necessary, add up to 1 more tablespoon warm water to adjust consistency).
3. Wrap dough in plastic wrap and set aside while preparing filling (plastic wrap will prevent dough from cracking).

To Prepare Filling:
1. In a 10-inch nonstick skillet, heat margarine until bubbly and hot.
2. Add vegetables and garlic and sauté over medium-low heat, stirring occasionally until vegetables are tender, about 3 minutes.
3. Set aside and let cool.
4. In large mixing bowl, combine rice, ricotta cheese, 3 egg whites, 2 tablespoons Parmesan cheese, salt and pepper; beat until smooth.
5. Add cooled vegetables and stir to combine.

To Prepare Torte:
1. Preheat oven to 350°F.
2. Between 2 sheets of wax paper, roll dough; forming a rectangle about 1/8-inch thick.
3. Remove paper and lift dough into a 10x6x2-inch baking dish so that edges of dough extend slightly over sides of dish.
4. Spoon cheese mixture over dough and bring up sides of dough over edges of filling, leaving center uncovered.
5. In a small bowl, beat remaining egg whites with remaining tablespoon Parmesan cheese.

Continued on following page.

Continued from preceding page.

6. Pour over entire surface of torte.
7. Bake until brown, about 1 hour.
8. Remove from oven and let stand until set, about 15 minutes.
9. Serve warm or at room temperature.

Yield: 8 servings
Per Serving:
207 cal, 7 gm fat, 10 gm pro, 26 gm carb, 11 mg chol, 215 mg sodium, 1 gm dietary fiber

Pesto Sauce   Chuck Coronado

4 c. fresh basil, rinsed &
  patted dry
3 T. olive oil
2 cloves garlic
2 T. parsley

1/2 tsp. salt
1/8 tsp. pepper
1/4 c. walnuts
1/2 c. Parmesan cheese

1. Place basil in bowl of food processor.
2. Pour remaining ingredients on top and process until all ingredients are combined.
3. Toss 1 tablespoon of sauce with 1 cup of your favorite cooked pasta.

Yield: 16 servings
Per Serving (1 tablespoon):
49 cal, 4 gm fat, 2 gm pro, 1 gm carb, 2 mg chol, 117 mg sodium, 0 gm fiber

Original Tomato Sauce
Nutrition Staff

1 tsp. minced garlic
1 T. olive oil
4 lb. fresh Italian roma
   tomatoes
1 sm. onion or shallot,
   chopped

1/2 pablano pepper, seeded
   & chopped
1/4 tsp. salt
1/2 green bell pepper,
   chopped (optional)
Tabasco sauce (optional)

1. Lightly brown garlic in olive oil.
2. Cut tomatoes in small chunks.
3. Add tomatoes to garlic along with onion, pablano pepper, salt and green pepper.
4. Cook on high until tomatoes soften, then lower heat and cook 20 minutes.
5. Add Tabasco sauce to taste.
6. Serve over your favorite pasta.

Yield: 6 servings
Per Serving (3/4 cup sauce):
   89 cal, 3 gm fat, 3 gm pro, 15 gm carb, 0 mg chol, 114 mg sodium, 4 gm dietary fiber

Italian Tomato Sauce
Nutrition Staff

2 (28 oz.) cans Italian
   tomatoes, crushed
1 tsp. basil
1/2 tsp. oregano

1 (6 oz.) can tomato paste
1 bay leaf
5 tsp. minced garlic
1/2 tsp. pepper

1. Mix all ingredients; simmer on stove for 2 hours.
2. Use in your favorite Italian recipe or serve over spaghetti.

Yield: 14 servings
Per Serving (1/2 cup):
   37 cal, 0 gm fat, 2 gm pro, 8 gm carb, 0 mg chol, 193 mg sodium, 2 gm dietary fiber

Marinara Sauce

Cindy Kleckner, R.D.

1 T. olive oil
1 tsp. minced garlic
4 (16 oz.) cans tomatoes,
   chopped & drained

2 (16 oz.) cans tomato
   sauce
2 tsp. crushed oregano
1 1/2 T. dried parsley

1. Heat olive oil in skillet; when hot, sauté garlic. Do not brown garlic.
2. Add chopped tomatoes and tomato sauce to skillet; stir in oregano and parsley.
3. Bring to a boil and simmer, covered, for 1 1/2 hours, stirring occasionally.
4. Serve over your favorite pasta.

Yield: 16 servings
Per Serving (1/2 cup):
   45 cal, 1 gm fat, 2 gm pro, 8 gm carb, 0 mg chol, 482 mg sodium, 2 gm dietary fiber

Homemade Meat Sauce

Nutrition Staff

12 oz. ground round
1 c. diced onion
1/2 green bell pepper
1/2 tsp. minced garlic
1 tsp. cinnamon
1/4 tsp. black pepper
1 (8 oz.) can tomato sauce,
   unsalted

1 (8 oz.) can mushroom
   stems & pieces, drained
2 T. worcestershire sauce
1 tsp. Italian seasoning
Nonstick vegetable
   cooking spray

1. In skillet, brown beef and drain off fat.
2. Transfer beef to colander and rinse under hot water. Pat dry with paper towels.
3. Sauté onion, green pepper and garlic until tender in pan sprayed with nonstick spray.
4. Return beef to skillet with vegetables and add cinnamon, pepper, tomato sauce, mushrooms, worcestershire sauce and Italian seasoning.
5. Bring mixture to a boil, then simmer gently for about 15 minutes.
6. Serve over your favorite pasta.

Yield: 6 servings
Per Serving:
   146 cal, 7 gm fat, 13 gm pro, 8 gm carb, 36 mg chol, 297 mg sodium, 2 gm dietary fiber

Easy Meat Sauce
Georgia Kostas, M.P.H., R.D.

8 oz. lean ground beef
8 oz. lean ground turkey
   breast
2 (16 oz.) cans spaghetti
   sauce

1 c. water
2 T. Italian herb season-
   ings blend

1. Heat skillet on stove for 3 to 5 minutes.
2. When hot, add ground meats and brown; drain off fat.
3. Add spaghetti sauce, water and seasonings.
4. Simmer 30 to 45 minutes.
5. Serve over spaghetti for a wonderful meal.

Yield: 6 servings
Per Serving (approximately 1/2 cup sauce):
   217 cal, 10 gm fat, 18 gm pro, 15 gm carb, 49 mg chol, 632 mg sodium,
   3 gm dietary fiber

Mexican Olé

Mexican Olé

Mexican Olé

Enchiladas Suisas
Veronica Coronado

1/2 T. margarine	5 oz. low-fat Cheddar
2 Spanish onions, chopped	cheese, grated (1 1/4 c.)
2 T. flour	2 scallions, chopped
1 1/2 c. chicken broth	12 (6") corn tortillas
2 (4 oz.) cans mild green	1 1/2 c. shredded, cooked
chilies, chopped	chicken
1/2 tsp. minced garlic	1 c. skim milk
1/4 tsp. cumin	1 c. cherry tomatoes,
3 oz. low-fat Monterey Jack	sliced in half
cheese, grated (3/4 c.)	Nonstick vegetable
	cooking spray

1. Spray a large skillet with cooking spray. Add the margarine and melt over medium heat. Add onion and sauté until soft, about 2 minutes.
2. Stir in the flour and chicken broth; add the chilies, garlic and cumin; simmer about 15 minutes to blend the flavors of the sauce.
3. Preheat oven to 350°F.
4. Lightly spray a rectangular baking dish with cooking spray.
5. Combine the cheeses and slice the scallions.
6. Dip corn tortillas in the sauce.
7. Put some of the chicken in a strip on each tortilla; top with 2 table-spoons cheese.
8. Roll up the enchiladas and put in the prepared baking dish seam-side down.
9. Pour the remaining sauce over them and then the milk.
10. Sprinkle with the remaining cheese and scallions.
11. Bake until hot and bubbly, about 20 minutes.
12. Serve hot, garnished with tomatoes.

NOTE: To make this dish in advance, follow directions, except adding milk. Add milk prior to baking. Can be made 2 days in advance.

Yield: 12 servings
Per Serving (1 enchilada):
195 cal, 6 gm fat, 16 gm pro, 20 gm carb, 29 mg chol, 300 mg sodium, 2 gm dietary fiber

One teaspoon of salt equals 2,300 mg of sodium.

Chicken Enchiladas with Green Chilies

Cindy Kleckner, R.D.

1 lb. fresh tomatillos; or 2 (13 oz.) cans tomatillos, drained
1 (7 oz.) can diced green chilies, undrained
1/2 T. vegetable oil
1 med. onion, finely chopped
1/2 tsp. minced garlic
1 (14 1/2 oz.) can chicken broth, low-sodium, defatted*
12 (6") corn tortillas

3 c. cooked chicken, shredded
1 c. (4 oz.) low-fat Monterey Jack cheese, shredded
1 1/2 c. (6 oz.) low-fat Cheddar cheese, shredded
6 T. light sour cream
4 green onions with tops, thinly sliced
Fresh cilantro sprigs for garnish (optional)

1. Preheat oven to 350°F.
2. If using fresh tomatillos, remove husks; wash thoroughly.
3. Place tomatillos in 2-quart pan and add 1/2-inch water; bring to a boil.
4. Cover; reduce heat and simmer 10 minutes or until tender; drain.
5. Place tomatillos and chilies in blender or food processor container fitted with metal blade; process until puréed.
6. Heat the 1/2 tablespoon vegetable oil in a large skillet over medium heat.
7. Add onion and garlic; cook until onion is tender.
8. Stir in purée and chicken broth; simmer uncovered until sauce has reduced to about 2 1/2 cups and has consistency of canned tomato sauce.
9. Dip tortilla into tomatillo sauce.
10. Transfer sauced tortillas to a plate. Combine Monterey Jack and Cheddar cheeses. Place about 1/4 cup of the chicken and 2 tablespoons cheese across center of tortillas; roll to enclose.
11. Place enchilada, seam-side down in a 15x10x2-inch baking pan.
12. Repeat until all tortillas are filled.
13. Spoon remaining sauce over enchiladas, making sure all ends are moistened; reserve remaining cheese; cover and bake 20 to 30 minutes or until hot in center.
14. Uncover and top with reserved cheese; continue baking, uncovered, 10 minutes or until cheese is melted.
15. Spoon sour cream down center of enchiladas; sprinkle with green onions; garnish with cilantro if desired.
  * To defat chicken broth, place canned broth in refrigerator; when cold skim fat off the top.

Yield: 12 servings
Per Serving (1 enchilada):
    234 cal, 8 gm fat, 23 mg pro, 18 gm carb, 49 mg chol, 243 mg sodium, 2 gm dietary fiber

Spicy Bean Enchiladas

Nutrition Staff

3/4 lb. dried pinto beans
8 c. water
1 tsp. minced garlic
1 bay leaf
3/4 tsp. salt
Spicy Tomato Sauce
    (See Recipe Following)
1/2 tsp. chili powder
1/4 tsp. pepper

8 (6") corn tortillas
1 c. (4 oz.) low-fat Cheddar
    cheese, shredded
1/2 c. plain nonfat yogurt
2 T. green onions, chopped
Shredded lettuce (optional)
Nonstick vegetable
    cooking spray

1. Sort and wash beans.
2. Cover with water 2 inches above top of beans, and let stand 8 hours; drain.
3. Combine beans, 8 cups water, garlic, bay leaf and salt in Dutch oven; bring to a boil.
4. Cover and reduce heat to medium; cook for 1 1/2 hours or until beans are tender.
5. Drain and discard bay leaf.
6. Mash beans; add 1/2 cup Spicy Tomato Sauce, chili powder and pepper; stirring well.
7. Spread 1/2 cup bean mixture over each tortilla. Roll up, place seam-side down in a 13x9x2-inch baking dish sprayed with cooking spray.
8. Spoon remaining Spicy Tomato Sauce over tortillas; cover and bake at 350°F. for 20 minutes.
9. Top with cheese and bake, uncovered an additional 5 minutes or until cheese melts.
10. Serve with a spoonful of yogurt, and sprinkle with green onions.
11. Garnish with lettuce, if desired.

NOTE: If corn tortillas crack or are hard to roll up, soften by steaming. To steam, place 2 to 3 tortillas at a time in a strainer, and place over boiling water. Cover and steam 2 to 3 minutes or until softened and pliable.

Yield: 8 servings
Per Serving (1 enchilada):
    290 cal, 4 gm fat, 17 gm pro, 48 gm carb, 9 mg chol, 366 mg sodium, 11 gm dietary fiber

One chicken enchilada with sour cream sauce from a Mexican restaurant contains approximately 320 calories and 18 grams of fat.

Spicy Tomato Sauce

Nutrition Staff

2 (8 oz.) cans tomato
sauce, no added salt
1 (4 oz.) can chopped
green chilies, un-
drained
1/2 tsp. minced garlic

3/4 c. green onions,
chopped
2 tsp. chili powder
1 tsp. ground cumin
1/4 tsp. dried whole
oregano

1. Combine all ingredients in a saucepan; simmer, uncovered, about 5 minutes.

Yield: 8 servings
Per Serving (4 tablespoons):
28 cal, 0 gm fat, 1 gm pro, 6 gm carb, 0 mg chol, 20 mg sodium, 1 gm dietary fiber

Tostadas

Nutrition Staff

8 (6") corn tortillas
2 c. lettuce, shredded
4 tomatoes, chopped
1 c. red onion, chopped
8 T. low-fat Cheddar cheese,
grated (1/2 c.)

8 T. plain nonfat yogurt
(1/2 c.)
2 c. Vegetarian Black Bean
Chili excluding toppings
(See Index)
Nonstick vegetable
cooking spray

1. Spray a cookie sheet with cooking spray. Place tortillas on prepared cookie sheet and brown on both sides in oven at 200°F.
2. Layer on top of each tortilla: 1/4 cup lettuce, 1/2 tomato, 2 tablespoons onion, 1/4 cup chili mixture, 1 tablespoon cheese and 1 tablespoon yogurt.

Yield: 8 servings
Per Serving (1 tostada):
184 cal, 3 gm fat, 10 gm pro, 31 gm carb, 5 mg chol, 129 mg sodium 4 gm dietary fiber

Red Snapper Veracruz
Nutrition Staff

4 (5 oz.) red snapper fillets
1 T. lime juice
2 green onions, minced
1/2 tsp. minced garlic
1/4 c. dry white wine
4 canned tomatoes,
    drained & chopped

3 T. fresh cilantro, chopped
1 1/2 tsp. oregano
1 1/2 tsp. thyme
1 tsp. Tabasco sauce
Nonstick vegetable
    cooking spray

1. Preheat oven to 350°F.
2. Spray a baking dish with cooking spray and place fillets in the dish. Sprinkle with lime juice.
3. Sauté onions and garlic in white wine over low heat.
4. Add tomatoes and Tabasco sauce; cook for 5 minutes.
5. Add herbs. Pour tomato mixture over fish; cover.
6. Bake 20 to 30 minutes. Use lime wedges and fresh cilantro for garnish.

Yield: 4 servings
Per Serving (1 fillet):
    163 cal, 2 gm fat, 29 gm pro, 4 gm carb, 51 mg chol, 141 mg sodium, 1 gm dietary fiber

Twelve large restaurant tortilla chips contain
approximately 300 calories and 16 grams of fat.

Mexican Lasagna   Barbara Bartolomeo

1 tsp. olive oil	1/2 green bell pepper,
8 oz. boneless, skinless	diced
chicken breasts, sliced	1 sm. onion, diced
in long, thin strips	2 T. cilantro, chopped
(oriental style)	1/2 tsp. minced garlic
1/2 red bell pepper, diced	

1. Sauté the above ingredients in the oil, stirring for about 10 minutes.

3/4 c. plain nonfat yogurt	1/2 c. part-skim mozzarella
3/4 c. part-skim ricotta	cheese, grated
cheese	

1. Mix the cheeses together.

1 (14 1/2 oz.) can Del Monte	1 tsp. cumin
Mexican stewed tomatoes	1 T. chili powder
1 (6 oz.) can tomato sauce	

1. Mix the above together.

8 (6") corn tortillas	Nonstick vegetable
	cooking spray

1. Spray a 9-inch square pan with cooking spray; line bottom with the tortillas (torn to fit the sides and corners).
2. Cover with a layer of sauce, then a layer of cheese and lastly, a layer of chicken mixture.
3. Repeat layering with tortillas, etc. Add a third layer of tortillas and sauce on top.
4. Bake at 350°F., covered, for 45 minutes.
5. Cut and serve.

Yield: 6 servings
Per Serving:
      268 cal, 8 gm fat, 21 gm pro, 30 gm carb, 40 mg chol, 524 mg sodium, 4 gm dietary fiber

Eat a variety of foods to maximize your nutrient intake.

Mexican Migas

Nutrition Staff

1/4 c. green onions,
 chopped
2 (6") corn tortillas, cut
 into 1" squares
1/2 c. chicken broth
1 tomato, chopped

1 1/2 c. egg substitute
2 oz. green chilies,
 chopped
1/4 tsp. pepper
1/8 tsp. salt

1. Sauté onions and tortillas in broth until onions are tender. Add tomatoes; heat.
2. Add egg substitute, chilies, pepper and salt to skillet.
3. Continue to cook, stirring until mixture is evenly cooked.
4. Serve immediately.

Yield: 4 servings
Per Serving:
 87 cal, 1 gm fat, 10 gm pro, 10 gm carb, 1 mg chol, 313 mg sodium, 1 gm dietary fiber

Mexican Bean Bake

Georgia Kostas, M.P.H., R.D.

6 (6") corn tortillas
2 c. cooked kidney beans
1 onion, chopped
1/2 tsp. minced garlic
1/8 tsp. pepper
1 T. basil
1 T. oregano
1 bouillon cube

1 T. parsley flakes
1 (15 oz.) can tomato
 sauce
1 (8 oz.) can tomato paste
1/2 c. part-skim ricotta
 cheese
4 oz. part-skim mozzarella
 cheese, shredded

1. Stir and heat in a saucepan the beans, onion, garlic, seasonings and bouillon cube.
2. Add tomato sauce and paste; cook 20 minutes, stirring constantly.
3. Add ricotta cheese; stir and heat.
4. Line bottom of an 11x7x2-inch baking pan with 6 tortillas.
5. Layer with bean mixture and then mozzarella cheese.
6. Bake, uncovered, at 400°F. for 30 minutes.

Yield: 6 servings
Per Serving:
 293 cal, 7 gm fat, 18 gm pro, 43 gm carb, 17 mg chol, 805 mg sodium, 9 gm dietary fiber

Pizza Olé

Cindy Kleckner, R.D.

1/2 c. plus 1 T. cornmeal
1 1/2 c. wholewheat flour
1 T. baking powder
1/2 tsp. salt (optional)
3/4 c. skim milk
3 T. vegetable oil
1 (12 oz.) jar taco sauce
1 (15 1/2 oz.) can Mexican-
style chili beans, un-
drained

1 green bell pepper, cut
into thin rings
6 oz. part-skim mozzarella
cheese, shredded
Nonstick vegetable
cooking spray

1. Preheat oven to 450°F.
2. Spray a 14-inch round pizza pan with cooking spray.
3. Sprinkle 1 tablespoon cornmeal evenly into prepared pan.
4. In a medium bowl, combine remaining 1/2 cup cornmeal, flour, baking powder and salt; add milk and oil.
5. Stir with fork until mixture forms a ball.
6. Press dough into prepared pan; shape edge to form rim.
7. Bake 15 minutes.
8. Spread taco sauce evenly over partially baked crust; top with beans, green pepper rings and cheese.
9. Continue baking 10 minutes or until cheese is melted.

Yield: 8 servings
Per Serving:
324 cal, 12 gm fat, 16 gm pro, 44 gm carb, 12 mg chol, 575 mg sodium, 7 gm dietary fiber

One gram of protein equals 4 calories.

Mexican Pizza Stacks   Cindy Kleckner, R.D.

1 (24 oz.) can black beans,
  drained & rinsed
1 (17 oz.) can corn or
  hominy, drained & rinsed
2 to 3 T. canned, chopped
  jalapeño peppers
6 (7") flour tortillas
2 oz. low-fat Cheddar
  cheese, shredded

1 (2 1/4 oz.) can sliced pitted ripe olives, drained
1 lg. tomato, cut into thin
  wedges
Light sour cream or salsa
  (optional)
1 sliced green onion
Nonstick vegetable
  cooking spray

1. Preheat oven to 375°F.
2. In a 2-quart saucepan stir together the black beans, corn or hominy and jalapeño peppers; cook and stir until heated through.
3. Spray a large baking sheet with nonstick spray. Place 2 of the tortillas side-by-side on the baking sheet. Spoon 2/3 cup of the black bean mixture onto each tortilla. Sprinkle each tortilla with about 2 teaspoons of the cheese and a few olives. Repeat layers twice.
4. Cover baking sheet loosely with foil. Bake in a 375°F. oven about 25 minutes or until hot. Cut into wedges; top with tomato, sour cream or salsa and onion. Makes 2 stacks.

Yield: 4 servings
Per Serving:
   280 cal, 5 gm fat, 14 gm pro, 49 gm carb, 5 mg chol, 540 mg sodium, 7 gm dietary fiber

In Brazil, jogging is called "doing the Cooper".

Mexican Salad

Jean Wisner, R.D.

SPICY DRESSING:

4 oz. btl. fat-free Italian
dressing

2 T. cilantro, chopped
1/4 c. salsa

SALAD:

4 c. salad greens, torn
2 med. tomatoes, cut into
wedges
1/4 c. green onions,
chopped

1/4 c. pitted ripe olives,
sliced
1/4 c. low-fat Cheddar
cheese, shredded
24 South of the Border
chips (See Index)

1. Combine dressing ingredients in blender until smooth; set aside.
2. Combine salad ingredients, except chips, and toss lightly.
3. Top with chips.
4. Drizzle dressing over top of salad.

Yield: 6 servings
Per Serving:

107 cal, 3 gm fat, 4 gm pro, 16 gm carb, 3 mg chol, 527 mg sodium,
2 gm dietary fiber

Gazpacho

Nutrition Staff

4 c. tomato juice, low-
sodium
1/2 c. cucumber, unpeeled
& chopped
1/4 c. green bell pepper,
chopped
1/4 c. onion, finely chopped
1/4 c. celery, finely chopped

1 T. olive oil
2 T. wine vinegar
1/2 tsp. pepper
1 tsp. oregano
1/4 tsp. basil
1/2 tsp. minced garlic

1. Combine all ingredients.
2. Cover and chill overnight.

Yield: 6 servings
Per Serving (3/4 cup):

46 cal, 1 gm fat, 2 gm pro, 9 gm carb, 0 mg chol, 21 mg sodium, 1 gm
dietary fiber

Refried Beans
Karen Angevine, R.D.

3 c. cooked pinto beans
1 T. vegetable oil
1/2 c. onion, chopped
1 tsp. minced garlic

Garlic powder, to taste
Cayenne pepper, to taste
Black pepper, to taste

1. Place pinto beans in a food processor and purée.
2. Heat oil in large skillet on medium-high heat. Add onions and garlic; sauté.
3. Pour puréed beans into the skillet. Stir beans until thickened.
4. Beans may be seasoned with spices while cooking.
5. Serve hot with your favorite Mexican dish.

Yield: 6 servings
Per Serving (1/2 cup):
228 cal, 3 gm fat, 12 gm pro, 40 gm carb, 0 mg chol, 0 mg sodium, 9 gm dietary fiber

Spanish Rice
Susie Costello

1/2 c. green bell pepper, chopped
1 c. onion, chopped
2 cloves garlic, minced
1 c. brown rice, uncooked
2 T. canola oil
1 (14 1/2 oz.) can tomatoes
1/4 c. water

2 T. red wine vinegar
1/4 tsp. salt
1/4 tsp. pepper
1 c. frozen green peas, thawed
1/2 c. low-fat Monterey Jack cheese, shredded

1. Sauté bell pepper, onion, garlic and rice in oil until rice is lightly browned.
2. Finely chop tomatoes; add tomatoes and juice, water, vinegar, salt and pepper to rice; cover.
3. Cook until rice is done.
4. Add peas, stirring well; pour mixture into a 1 1/2-quart baking dish.
5. Top with cheese and bake at 400°F. until cheese melts.

Yield: 12 servings
Per Serving (1/2 cup):
113 cal, 4 gm fat, 4 gm pro, 17 gm carb, 3 mg chol, 139 mg sodium, 2 gm dietary fiber

South of the Border Chips

Jean Wisner, R.D.

7 flour tortillas, cut into
   6 pieces
1 tsp. garlic powder

Nonstick vegetable cooking
   spray

1. Preheat oven to 350°F.
2. Generously coat a large cookie sheet with cooking spray.
3. Lay tortilla pieces flat on pan so that all pieces are exposed.
4. Spray all strips generously with cooking spray.
5. Sprinkle with garlic powder.
6. Bake 12 to 16 minutes until lightly browned.

NOTE: If edges of tortilla pieces start to curl up, place another cookie sheet over the tortillas as they bake.

Yield: 7 servings
Per Serving (6 chips):
   86 cal, 2 gm fat, 3 gm pro, 15 gm carb, 0 mg chol, 155 mg sodium,
   1 gm dietary fiber

Salsa

Nutrition Staff

1 to 4 whole jalapeño
   peppers, to taste, diced
2 tomatoes, chopped
1 (1 lb.) can chopped tomatoes,
   undrained

1/4 tsp. ground cumin
1/4 tsp. cayenne pepper

1. Combine pepper, tomatoes, canned tomatoes and seasonings.
2. Chill.

Yield: 16 servings
Per Serving (1/4 cup):
   10 cal, 0 gm fat, 0 gm pro, 2 gm carb, 0 mg chol, 63 mg sodium, 0 gm
   dietary fiber

Mango Tomato Salsa
Jean Wisner, R.D.

1 ripe mango, cut into 1/4"
cubes
1 yellow tomato, cut into
1/4" cubes
2 sm. red tomatoes, cut
into 1/4" cubes

1/2 c. green onions,
chopped
1/4 c. cilantro, chopped
1/2 tsp. garlic powder
1 T. lime juice

1. Toss all ingredients together lightly.
2. Serve in a glass bowl or southwestern style crock.
3. Serve with South of the Border Chips (See Index).

Yield: 12 servings
Per Serving (1/4 cup):
   16 cal, 0 fat, 0 gm pro, 4 gm carb, 0 mg chol, 3 mg sodium, 1 gm dietary
   fiber

Mexican Bean Dip
Nutrition Staff

3/4 c. cooked pinto beans
2 T. picante sauce

1/2 tsp. lime juice

1. Put all ingredients in blender.
2. Process until smooth.
3. Chill; serve with Pita Crackers (See Index).

Yield: 14 servings
Per Serving (1 tablespoon):
   23 cal, 0 gm fat, 1 gm pro, 4 gm carb, 0 mg chol, 11 mg sodium, 1 gm
   dietary fiber

Notes and Recipes

Beginning
the
Day

Beginning the Day

Beginning the Day

Sunrise Pancake Stack
Cindy Kleckner, R.D.

1 1/2 c. wholewheat flour
2 tsp. baking powder
1 tsp. orange peel, grated
1 egg white
2 1/2 T. honey
1/4 c. skim milk

3/4 c. orange juice
1 T. vegetable oil
1 1/2 c. part-skim ricotta cheese
Nonstick vegetable cooking spray

1. In a medium bowl, combine flour, baking powder and orange peel.
2. In a separate bowl, combine egg white, honey, milk, orange juice and oil.
3. Stir the wet ingredients into the dry ingredients just enough to moisten.
4. Cook four large pancakes on a griddle sprayed with cooking spray.
5. Spread 1/2 cup ricotta cheese between each pancake.
6. Cut into 6 wedges and serve with low-calorie syrup.

Yield: 6 servings
Per Serving (1 wedge):
254 cal, 8 gm fat, 12 gm pro, 36 gm carb, 19 mg chol, 228 mg sodium, 4 gm dietary fiber

Oatmeal Pancakes
Nutrition Staff

1 1/2 c. oatmeal, dry
2 c. low-fat buttermilk
2 egg whites

1 c. wholewheat flour
2 tsp. baking soda
1 banana, mashed

1. Combine oatmeal, buttermilk and egg whites; let stand for at least 1/2 hour or refrigerate up to 24 hours.
2. Add remaining ingredients; stir the batter just until dry ingredients are moistened.
3. Bake on a hot, lightly oiled griddle.

Yield: 12 small pancakes, each 5 inches across
Per Serving (1 pancake):
98 cal, 1 gm fat, 5 gm pro, 18 gm carb, 1 mg chol, 189 mg sodium, 2 gm dietary fiber

Wholegrain Pancakes

Nutrition Staff

2/3 c. wholewheat flour,
    stone-ground
1/3 c. flour
1/4 c. oatmeal, dry
2 T. wheat germ
2 tsp. sugar
1 tsp. baking powder

1/2 tsp. baking soda
1/8 tsp. salt (optional)
3 egg whites
1 c. low-fat buttermilk
1/4 c. skim milk (more if
    mixture is too dry)
1 T. vegetable oil

1. Mix together all dry ingredients in a medium bowl.
2. In a separate bowl, beat egg whites until fluffy; set aside.
3. In a third bowl, combine buttermilk, skim milk and oil, folding in egg whites; add to the dry ingredients, stirring just to combine them.
4. Let the batter stand for about 10 minutes; bake on a hot, lightly oiled griddle.

Yield: 12 small pancakes (5-inch)
Per Serving (1 pancake):
    71 cal, 2 gm fat, 4 gm pro, 11 gm carb, 1 mg chol, 105 mg sodium, 1 gm dietary fiber

Breakfast eaters consume more essential nutrients...calcium, fiber, Vitamin C, thiamine and riboflavin...than do breakfast skippers.

French Toast Puff

Nutrition Staff

1 c. egg substitute
1/2 c. evaporated skimmed
   milk
1 T. honey
1/2 tsp. cinnamon
1/2 tsp. mace

4 (1 oz.) slices cinnamon-
   raisin bread, cut diagonally in half
Nonstick vegetable
   cooking spray

GARNISH (OPTIONAL):
Powdered sugar

Berry Syrup (See Index)

1. Spray a 9-inch pie plate with cooking spray.
2. In medium bowl, whisk together all ingredients except bread and garnish.
3. Place bread in prepared plate; pour milk mixture over bread.
4. Cover with plastic wrap; refrigerate at least 1 hour or overnight.
5. Preheat oven to 350°F. Bake 25 to 30 minutes until puffy and golden brown.
6. Garnish with powdered sugar or serve with Berry Syrup.
7. Serve immediately.

Yield: 4 servings
Per Serving (1 slice):
   141 cal, 1 gm fat, 9 gm pro, 24 gm carb, 2 mg chol, 219 mg sodium, 1 gm dietary fiber

Berry Syrup

Nutrition Staff

2 c. berries (blueberries,
   strawberries, rasp-
   berries)

2 T. fruit juice
1/2 tsp. vanilla

1. Process berries in a food processor.
2. Combine all ingredients in a heavy saucepan.
3. Bring to a boil and simmer 25 to 30 minutes.

Yield: 1/2 cup
Per Serving (1 tablespoon):
   19 cal, 0 gm fat, 0 gm pro, 5 gm carb, 0 mg chol, 1 mg sodium, 1 gm dietary fiber

Ham and Egg Casserole

Edna Ground

1 1/2 c. egg substitute
2 c. skim milk
1 c. low-fat sharp Cheddar
   cheese, shredded
1 tsp. mustard

3 slices wholewheat bread
12 oz. turkey ham, cut into
   small pieces
Nonstick vegetable
   cooking spray

1. Combine egg substitute, milk, cheese and mustard; set aside.
2. Spray 12x9x2-inch baking dish with cooking spray; cover bottom of dish with torn bread.
3. Spread turkey ham over bread.
4. Pour egg mixture over turkey ham; cover with plastic wrap and refrigerate overnight.
5. Bake at 350°F. for 45 minutes or until knife inserted in the middle comes out clean.

Yield: 8 servings
Per Serving:
   161 cal, 5 gm fat, 19 gm pro, 9 gm carb, 42 mg chol, 646 mg sodium, 1 gm dietary fiber

Seafood Quiche

Nutrition Staff

1/2 c. egg substitute
4 egg whites, beaten well
6 oz. cooked shrimp
6 oz. crab meat
2 green onions, chopped
10 to 12 med. mushrooms,
   thinly sliced (approx.
   4 oz.)

1 1/4 c. evaporated
   skimmed milk
2 c. part-skim mozzarella
   or low-fat Swiss cheese,
   grated
Nonstick vegetable
   cooking spray

1. Mix all ingredients and pour into a 9x9x2-inch pan sprayed with cooking spray.
2. Bake at 350°F. for 30 to 40 minutes until firm and lightly browned.

Yield: 8 servings
Per Serving:
   171 cal, 6 gm fat, 23 gm pro, 7 gm carb, 71 mg chol, 350 mg sodium, 0 gm dietary fiber

Zucchini Quiche

Cindy Kleckner, R.D.

CRUST:
1 T. active dry yeast
1/2 c. warm water

1/2 c. wholewheat flour
3/4 c. flour
1/4 tsp. salt

1. Dissolve yeast in water.
2. Stir in flour and salt.
3. Knead dough on floured board for 5 minutes until smooth and elastic.
4. Let rise for 45 minutes.

FILLING:
2 tsp. margarine
4 c. unpeeled zucchini,
   thinly sliced
1 c. onion, coarsely
   chopped
3 T. fresh parsley, chopped
1/4 tsp. salt

1/2 tsp. pepper
1/2 tsp. garlic powder
1/2 tsp. basil
1/2 tsp. oregano
3 egg whites
2 c. part-skim mozzarella
   cheese, grated
2 1/2 tsp. brown mustard

1. Preheat oven to 375°F.
2. Heat margarine in a large skillet and add zucchini and onion; cook until tender, about 10 minutes.
3. Stir in parsley and seasonings; set aside.
4. In a large bowl, blend egg whites and cheese.
5. Stir into vegetable mixture.
6. Transfer raised dough to an ungreased 10-inch pie pan.
7. Press over bottom and up sides to form crust.
8. Spread mustard over crust.
9. Pour vegetable mixture evenly over crust.
10. Bake for 25 to 35 minutes or until knife inserted near center comes out clean.
11. If crust becomes too brown, cover with foil during last 10 minutes of baking.
12. Let quiche stand 10 minutes before serving.

Yield: 4 servings
Per Serving (1/4 pie):
   369 cal, 13 gm fat, 25 gm pro, 41 gm carb, 30 mg chol, 677 mg sodium, 4 gm dietary fiber

Choose breads, cereals and crackers that
contain 2 grams of fat or less per serving.

Quick and Easy Quiche

Brenda Mack

1/3 c. onion, chopped
5 oz. Canadian bacon,
   chopped
1 c. low-fat Swiss cheese,
   shredded
1/3 c. green pepper,
   chopped

1/2 c. Bisquick
1 c. egg substitute
2 c. skim milk
1/8 tsp. salt
1/8 tsp. pepper
Nonstick vegetable
   cooking spray

1. Spray pie or quiche pan with cooking spray. Sprinkle with onion, Canadian bacon, Swiss cheese and green pepper.
2. Mix the Bisquick, egg substitute, milk, salt and pepper in a blender for 1 minute.
3. Pour mixture into pan.
4. Bake in oven preheated to 350°F. for 50 to 55 minutes or until center is set.
5. Let stand 5 minutes before cutting.

Yield: 8 servings
Per Serving:
   143 cal, 5 gm fat, 14 gm pro, 10 gm carb, 19 mg chol, 551 mg sodium, 0 gm dietary fiber

To mix frozen concenrated fruit juice quickly, remove from
can, place in pitcher and heat in the microwave
for 30 to 45 seconds until soft; add water.

Vegetable Quiche

Brenda Mack

CRUST:
2/3 c. flour
1/8 tsp. salt

2 T. shortening
1/3 c. low-fat cottage
cheese, sieved

QUICHE:
1 (10 oz.) pkg. chopped,
frozen broccoli or
spinach, cooked &
drained
1/4 c. green onion, finely-
chopped
1/2 c. part-skim mozzarella
cheese, shredded

1/2 c. low-fat Cheddar
cheese, shredded
3/4 c. egg substitute
1 c. evaporated skimmed
milk
1/8 tsp. salt
1/8 tsp. pepper
Sautéed onions, garlic,
shallots & parsley (optional)

1. Preheat oven to 325°F.
2. In a small bowl, combine flour and salt; cut in shortening until pieces are the size of small peas.
3. Add cottage cheese; toss mixture with fork until entire mixture is moistened.
4. Form dough into a ball.
5. Flatten on a very lightly floured surface by pressing with edge of hands 3 times across in both directions.
6. Roll out to 1/8-inch thickness.
7. Fit into a 9-inch pie plate or quiche pan; flute edges and set aside.
8. In small bowl, combine broccoli and onion.
9. In cottage cheese pastry shell, layer half the mozzarella and Cheddar cheese and the entire vegetable mixture.
10. In large bowl, combine egg substitute, evaporated skimmed milk, salt and pepper; pour egg mixture over vegetables in pastry shell.
11. Sprinkle with remaining mozzarella and Cheddar cheese.
12. Bake for 45 to 50 minutes or until knife inserted in center comes out clean.
13. Remove from oven and let stand 10 minutes before serving. (Texture may be soft.)

Yield: 8 servings
Per Serving:
154 cal, 6 gm fat, 12 gm pro, 14 gm carb, 10 mg chol, 256 mg sodium, 1 gm dietary fiber

Crustless Kale Pie

Cindy Kleckner, R.D.

4 tsp. diet margarine
2 med. onions, sliced
1 garlic clove, minced
2 (10 oz.) pkg. (4 c.) frozen
   chopped kale, thawed
3/4 c. egg substitute

1 1/2 c. evaporated
   skimmed milk
3 oz. part-skim mozzarella
   cheese, shredded
1/2 tsp. pepper
1/2 tsp. salt
Nonstick vegetable
   cooking spray

1. Preheat oven to 350°F.
2. Spray a 10-inch pie plate with cooking spray.
3. Melt margarine in medium skillet over medium-high heat; sauté onion and garlic until tender and remove from heat.
4. Squeeze thawed kale to remove all excess liquid.
5. Stir kale into onion mixture and combine; spread evenly in pie plate.
6. In a separate bowl, combine egg substitute, evaporated milk, mozzarella cheese, salt and pepper.
7. Pour into prepared pie plate, stirring to combine.
8. Bake 30 minutes, until center is almost set.
9. Let cool 10 minutes before serving.

Yield: 6 servings
Per Serving:
149 cal, 4 gm fat, 13 gm pro, 15 gm carb, 10 mg chol, 420 mg sodium, 5 gm dietary fiber

*Skipping breakfast to lose weight often leads
to overindulging later in the day.*

Breakfast Sundae

Nutrition Staff

6 T. raisins
6 T. water
1/2 T. almond extract
2 T. apple juice concen-
    trate, undiluted

3 c. low-fat cottage cheese
3 bananas, sliced
3 oranges, sliced
Favorite dry cereal (optional)

1. Combine raisins, water, almond extract and apple juice concentrate; let stand overnight.
2. In morning, bring mixture to a boil. Reduce heat, cover and let simmer 10 minutes.
3. For each serving, place 1/2 cup cottage cheese on serving plate.
4. Divide sliced fruit evenly among servings. Spoon raisin mixture over each.
5. Top with 3 tablespoons favorite dry cereal if desired.

Yield: 6 servings
Per Serving:
    205 cal, 2 gm fat, 16 gm pro, 34 gm carb, 12 mg chol, 461 mg sodium, 3 gm dietary fiber

Cheese Danish Rolls

Nutrition Staff

1 wholewheat English muffin
4 T. part-skim ricotta cheese

1/2 c. unsweetened apple-
    sauce
1 tsp. cinnamon

1. Preheat oven on broil.
2. In a toaster, toast English muffin halves lightly.
3. Top English muffin halves with ricotta cheese and applesauce.
4. Sprinkle with cinnamon; broil 2 to 3 minutes until cheese melts.

Yield: 1 serving
Per Serving:
    279 cal, 6 gm fat, 13 gm pro, 47 gm carb, 19 mg chol, 381 mg sodium, 6 gm dietary fiber

Granola

Kim Rojohn, R.D.

1 c. raisins
4 c. oatmeal, dry
1 c. bran flakes
2 c. All-Bran
1 1/2 tsp. cinnamon
1/2 tsp. nutmeg

1 c. orange juice
1/2 c. wheat germ (optional)
2 T. vanilla
1 apple, peeled & chopped
1/4 c. brown sugar
1/4 tsp. salt

1. Soak raisins in water for 15 minutes; drain.
2. Combine all ingredients. Spread thinly on 2 cookie sheets.
3. Bake 35 to 45 minutes at 350°F., until crunchy.

Yield: 18 servings
Per Serving (1/2 cup):
152 cal, 2 gm fat, 5 gm pro, 30 gm carb, 0 mg chol, 137 mg sodium,
6 gm dietary fiber

Fresh
from the Oven
Breads
& Muffins

Fresh from the Oven Breads & Muffins

Fresh from the Oven Breads & Muffins

Marvelous Oatmeal Muffins

Patty Kirk, R.D.

1 c. oatmeal, dry
1 c. low-fat buttermilk
1/4 c. margarine
1/4 c. egg substitute or
   2 egg whites
1/2 c. brown sugar

3/4 c. flour
1/4 c. wholewheat flour
1/2 tsp. baking soda
1 tsp. salt
Nonstick vegetable
   cooking spray

1. Combine oatmeal and buttermilk; soak for 1 hour and set aside.
2. Mix margarine, egg substitute or egg whites, and brown sugar together thoroughly.
3. Sift together flours, soda and salt; stir in, alternating with oatmeal and buttermilk mixture.
4. Fill muffin tins that have been sprayed with cooking spray 2/3 full.
5. Bake until golden brown at 400°F. for 15 to 20 minutes.

Yield: 15 muffins
Per Serving (1 muffin):
   111 cal, 3 gm fat, 3 gm pro, 17 gm carb, 0 mg chol, 230 mg sodium, 1 gm dietary fiber

One medium egg yolk contains 213 mg cholesterol.
Limit egg yolks to 0-3 a week.

Carrot Bran Muffins
Tricia Cox

2 1/2 c. bran flakes
1 1/4 c. skim milk
1/3 c. diet margarine
1 egg, beaten; or 2 egg
   whites
1 1/4 c. wholewheat flour
1/4 c. wheat bran

1/2 c. carrots, grated
1/4 c. raisins
1/3 c. sugar
1 T. baking powder
1/2 tsp. salt
Nonstick vegetable
   cooking spray

1. Combine cereal and milk; let stand for 5 minutes.
2. Add margarine and egg; mix well.
3. Add remaining ingredients, mixing just until moistened.
4. Spoon into muffin pan sprayed with cooking spray.
5. Bake at 400°F. for 25 minutes.

Yield: 12 muffins
Per Serving (1 muffin):
   141 cal, 3 gm fat, 4 gm pro, 25 gm carb, 18 mg chol, 345 mg sodium,
   4 gm dietary fiber

Carrot Oatmeal Muffins
Gail Brosey

1 c. buttermilk, skim
1 c. dry oatmeal
1/4 c. brown sugar
2 egg whites or 1/4 c. egg
   substitute
1 c. carrots, finely grated
1/2 c. raisins

1 tsp. cinnamon
1/2 c. applesauce
1/4 c. nonfat plain yogurt
   (optional)
1/2 c. oat bran, dry
1 c. wholewheat flour
1 tsp. baking soda

1. Mix buttermilk and oatmeal and let stand until liquid is absorbed.
2. Add sugar, egg whites, carrots, raisins, cinnamon, applesauce and
   yogurt (if desired). Mix well.
3. Stir together remaining dry ingredients and mix with wet ingredients.
4. Spray muffin tins with cooking spray and fill 2/3 full.
5. Bake at 375°F. for about 22 minutes.

Yield: 12 servings
Per Serving (1 muffin):
   132 cal, 1 gm fat, 5 gm pro, 28 gm carb, 0 mg chol, 104 mg sodium,
   3 gm dietary fiber

Applesauce Oatmeal Muffins

Juanita Hermon

1 1/2 c. oatmeal, dry
1 1/4 c. bran flakes, finely crushed
3/4 tsp. cinnamon
3/4 tsp. baking soda
3 T. vegetable oil

1 egg white
1 tsp. baking powder
1 c. unsweetened applesauce
1/2 c. skim milk
1/2 c. brown sugar

1. Preheat oven to 400°F.
2. Combine all ingredients.
3. Line muffin tins with paper muffin cups.
4. Divide batter equally (12 muffins).
5. Bake for 20 minutes or until tested done.

Yield: 12 muffins
Per Serving (1 muffin):
131 cal, 4 gm fat, 3 gm pro, 22 gm carb, 0 mg chol, 132 mg sodium, 2 gm dietary fiber

Mini Oat Bran Muffins

Nutrition Staff

1 1/4 c. oat bran, dry
1 c. wholewheat flour
1/3 c. raisins
1 T. baking powder
1/2 c. skim milk
1/2 c. orange juice

1/4 c. honey
2 T. vegetable oil
3 egg whites
Nonstick vegetable cooking spray

1. Preheat oven to 425°F.
2. Mix together dry ingredients.
3. Add skim milk, orange juice, honey, oil and egg whites; mix just until dry ingredients are moistened.
4. Divide mixture into mini muffin pans sprayed with cooking spray. Bake for 15 minutes or until lightly browned.

Yield: 24 muffins
Per Serving (1 muffin):
67 cal, 2 gm fat, 2 gm pro, 12 gm carb, 0 mg chol, 60 mg sodium, 1 gm dietary fiber

Refrigerator Bran Muffins

Susan Hoobler

4 c. All-Bran cereal
2 c. 100% Bran cereal
2 c. boiling water
1 c. raisins
1 c. dates
1 qt. low-fat buttermilk
3/4 c. safflower oil
1 c. molasses

1/2 c. brown sugar
2 eggs plus 4 egg whites
5 c. wholewheat flour
5 tsp. baking soda
5 tsp. cinnamon
Nonstick vegetable
    cooking spray

1. Pour boiling water over cereals, raisins and dates; let mixture cool.
2. Add buttermilk to bran mixture.
3. Cream oil, molasses and sugar.
4. Add eggs to creamed mixture; beat until fluffy.
5. Add creamed mixture to bran mixture.
6. Sift flour, baking soda and cinnamon; add to above batter and mix well.
7. Batter may be refrigerated for up to 4 weeks. When ready to bake muffins, spray muffin tins with cooking spray and fill each tin 2/3 full.
8. Bake at 375°F. for 20 to 25 minutes.

Yield: 48 servings
Per Serving (1 muffin):
   155 cal, 4 gm fat, 5 gm pro, 32 gm carb, 9 mg chol, 214 mg sodium, 6 gm dietary fiber

*To lower cholesterol in a recipe, substitute 2 egg whites
or 1/4 cup egg substitute for 1 whole egg.*

Pick Your Own Fruit or Vegetable Bran Muffins

Paula Nyman, R.D.

3 c. 100% Bran cereal
3 c. skim milk
2 egg whites
2 T. vegetable oil
2 3/4 c. wholewheat flour
1 c. sugar
2 T. baking powder
1 tsp. baking soda
1/2 tsp. salt
2 tsp. cinnamon

1/2 tsp. nutmeg
1 1/2 c. fruit or vegetable
of choice (mashed
bananas, grated apples,
blueberries, grated
zucchini, grated carrots,
crushed pineapple, etc.)
Nonstick vegetable
cooking spray

1. Combine bran flakes, milk, egg whites and oil; soak for 5 minutes.
2. Add to wet mixture the rest of the ingredients; stir by hand until well blended.
3. Spray muffin tins with cooking spray or use paper liners and fill tins 2/3 full of batter.
4. Bake in preheated 400°F. oven for approximately 20 minutes or until done.

Yield: 24 muffins
Per Serving (1 muffin without fruit or vegetable):
126 cal, 2 gm fat, 5 gm pro, 30 gm carb, 1 mg chol, 298 mg sodium, 6 gm dietary fiber

Put frozen bread loaves in a clean brown paper bag and place in 325° oven for 5 minutes to thaw completely.

Wholewheat Banana Nut Bread

Gail Brosey

1/4 c. vegetable oil
1/2 c. sugar
1/2 c. egg substitute; or
    4 egg whites
5 med. bananas (1 1/2 c.),
    mashed

2 c. wholewheat flour
1 T. baking powder
1/2 c. walnuts, chopped
Nonstick vegetable
    cooking spray

1. Preheat oven to 350°F.
2. Cream oil and sugar.
3. Add egg substitute or egg whites; beat 3 to 5 minutes.
4. Stir in bananas.
5. Blend in flour and baking powder.
6. Stir in walnuts; pour into a 9x5-inch loaf pan sprayed with cooking spray.
7. Bake for 75 minutes.

Yield: 20 servings
Per Serving (1 slice):
    130 cal, 5 gm fat, 3 gm pro, 21 gm carb, 0 mg chol, 70 mg sodium, 2 gm dietary fiber

Let nut breads and other quick breads stand for 10 minutes before removing from the pan to allow them to become firmer. Do not cool completely in the pan or they will become soggy.

Raspberry Nut Bread
Veronica Coronado

3 c. flour
2 c. sugar
3 tsp. cinnamon
1 tsp. baking soda
3/4 tsp. salt
1 (20 oz.) pkg. frozen raspberries, thawed & juice
   reserved

1 c. egg substitute; or 8
   egg whites
1/2 c. vegetable oil
1/2 c. walnuts, chopped
Nonstick vegetable
   cooking spray

1. Preheat oven to 350°F.
2. Mix flour, sugar, cinnamon, soda and salt together; make a well in the center.
3. Mash raspberries well; add egg substitute or egg whites and oil.
4. Combine with flour mixture; mix well. If batter appears too dry, add reserved juice.
5. Stir in nuts.
6. Pour into two 9x5x3-inch loaf pans sprayed with cooking spray and lightly floured.
7. Bake 1 hour. Let loaves cool completely before wrapping.

Yield: 2 loaves (16 slices/loaf)
Per Serving (1 slice):
   139 cal, 5 gm fat, 2 gm pro, 23 carb, 0 mg chol, 86 mg sodium, 2 gm dietary fiber

After rolls have baked, remove from pan immediately to
prevent steam from forming and making them heavy.

Strawberry Nut Bread
Jay Wilson

1 1/2 c. fresh strawberries;
  or frozen unsweetened
  & defrosted strawberries
1 3/4 c. flour
1 tsp. baking soda
1/4 tsp. baking powder
3/4 tsp. salt
1/2 tsp. cinnamon
1 c. sugar

1/4 c. vegetable oil
1/2 c. egg substitute or
  4 egg whites
1/3 c. water
1/4 c. walnuts, chopped
2 c. fresh strawberries
  (optional)
Nonstick vegetable
  cooking spray

1. Purée 1 1/2 cups strawberries in blender to yield 1 cup.
2. Combine flour, baking soda, baking powder, salt and cinnamon in a large mixing bowl.
3. Blend sugar, oil and egg substitute until light and fluffy.
4. Alternately add flour mixture and water to creamed mixture, mixing at low speed of electric mixer.
5. Stir in puréed strawberries; fold in walnuts.
6. Spread batter in a 9x5-inch loaf pan that has been sprayed with cooking spray.
7. Bake at 350°F. for about 1 hour or until toothpick inserted in center comes out clean.
8. Cool in pan 10 minutes; remove from pan and cool completely on wire rack.
9. Slice bread into 16 servings and serve with fresh strawberries if desired.

Yield: 16 servings
Per Serving (1 slice):
  141 cal, 5 gm fat, 2 gm pro, 23 gm carb, 0 mg chol, 168 mg sodium, 1 gm dietary fiber

*If an athletic event is greater than 2 hours in length, consume
small amounts of food and liquids every 15 to 30 minutes.
Try bananas, oranges, seedless grapes, figs, fig bars, raisins,
candy (no peanuts or chocolate), or water-diluted sugar drinks.*

Blueberry Yogurt Muffins

Veronica Coronado

2 c. flour
2 tsp. baking powder
1 tsp. baking soda
1/2 tsp. salt
3/4 c. brown sugar
1 c. plain nonfat yogurt

1/2 egg substitute or 4
   egg whites
1/4 c. margarine
2 c. fresh or frozen blueberries
Nonstick vegetable cooking
   spray

1. Preheat oven to 400°F.
2. Combine flour, baking powder, soda, salt and brown sugar.
3. Add yogurt, egg substitute or egg whites, and margarine.
4. Stir until flour is moistened; fold in blueberries.
5. Spoon into muffin tins sprayed with cooking spray.
6. Bake 20 to 25 minutes.

Yield: 18 muffins
Per Serving (1 muffin):
   124 cal, 3 gm fat, 3 gm pro, 23 gm carb, 0 mg chol, 202 mg sodium,
   1 gm dietary fiber

Pumpkin Muffins

Debby Wallace

2/3 c. nonfat dry powdered
   milk
2 tsp. pumpkin pie spice
1 tsp. cinnamon
6 T. flour
1 tsp. baking soda
1/4 c. sugar

1/2 c. egg substitute; or
   4 egg whites
1 T. vanilla extract
1 c. canned pumpkin
4 T. raisins
1/2 c. carrots, grated
Nonstick vegetable
   cooking spray

1. Preheat oven to 350°F.
2. Combine all ingredients; mix together.
3. Divide batter evenly into a 12-muffin tin that has been sprayed with cooking spray or lined with paper muffin cups.
4. Bake for approximately 20 minutes or until lightly browned.

Optional: May glaze muffins with a mixture of powdered sugar and milk. Use enough of each to make glaze a spreading consistency.

Yield: 12 servings
Per Serving (1 muffin without glaze):
   80 cal, 0 gm fat, 4 gm pro, 12 gm carb, 1 mg chol, 121 mg sodium,
   1 gm dietary fiber

Applesauce Bread

Veronica Coronado

1 c. applesauce, unsweet-
 ened
1 c. sugar
1/4 c. vegetable oil
4 egg whites
3 T. skim milk
1/2 c. raisins
1 c. flour

1 c. wholewheat flour
1 tsp. baking soda
1/2 tsp. baking powder
3/4 tsp. cinnamon
1/4 tsp. salt
1/2 tsp. nutmeg
Nonstick vegetable
 cooking spray

TOPPING (Optional):
2 T. pecans, chopped

1/2 c. brown sugar
1/2 tsp. cinnamon

1. Preheat oven to 350°F.
2. Combine applesauce, sugar, oil, egg whites, milk and raisins.
3. Sift together flours, baking soda, baking powder, cinnamon, salt and nutmeg.
4. Stir flour into applesauce mixture and mix well.
5. Pour into loaf pan sprayed with cooking spray.
6. Combine pecans, brown sugar and cinnamon; sprinkle over batter.
7. Bake for 1 hour.

Yield: 16 servings
Per Serving (1 slice without topping):
 152 cal, 4 gm fat, 3 gm pro, 29 gm carb, 0 mg chol, 113 mg sodium, 2 gm dietary fiber

For weight maintenance, men should consume approximately 2000 calories a day and women approximately 1500 calories a day.

Chocolate Cherry Muffins

Veronica Coronado

2 c. flour
1/2 c. sugar
3 1/2 T. cocoa powder
1 T. baking powder
1/2 tsp. salt
1/4 c. egg substitute; or
   2 egg whites

1 c. skim milk
1/4 c. vegetable oil
2 1/2 c. fresh or frozen
   unsweetened cherries,
   unthawed

1. Preheat oven to 400°F.
2. In a large mixing bowl, stir together flour, sugar, cocoa powder, baking powder and salt; set aside.
3. In a small bowl, mix egg substitute or egg whites, milk and oil.
4. Make a well in the flour mixture and pour in liquids; stir just until moistened (there may be a few lumps).
5. Fold in cherries; spoon into paper-lined muffin cups.
6. Bake for 20 to 25 minutes.

Yield: 12 servings
Per Serving (1 muffin):
   172 cal, 5 gm fat, 4 gm pro, 21 gm carb, 0 mg chol, 216 sodium, 2 gm dietary fiber

One teaspoon of soy sauce contains 1,029 mg sodium.

Poppyseed Dessert Bread

Patty Kirk, R.D.

3/4 c. egg substitute; or
   6 egg whites
2 1/2 c. sugar
1/2 c. vegetable oil
1 1/2 c. skim milk
1 1/2 tsp. vanilla extract
1 1/2 tsp. almond extract

3 c. flour
1 1/2 tsp. baking powder
1 1/2 tsp. poppy seeds
1 1/2 tsp. salt
Nonstick vegetable
   cooking spray

GLAZE TOPPING:
2 T. margarine, melted
3/4 c. sugar

1/4 c. orange juice
1/2 tsp. vanilla extract
1/2 tsp. almond extract

1. Spray 2 loaf pans with cooking spray and lightly coat with flour.
2. In a large bowl, cream egg substitute (or egg whites) and sugar.
3. Blend in oil, milk and extracts.
4. In a separate bowl, combine flour, baking powder, poppy seeds and salt.
5. Add flour mixture to wet mixture and stir to combine.
6. Pour into pans and bake for 1 hour at 325°F.
7. Combine all ingredients for glaze and heat.
8. When bread has cooled for 10 minutes, remove from pan and top with glaze.
9. Allow bread to cool completely, and cover with plastic wrap. Share with your friends.

Yield: 16 slices/loaf (2 loaves)
Per Serving (1 slice):
   159 cal, 4 gm fat, 2 gm pro, 30 gm carb, 0 mg chol, 141 mg sodium, 0 gm dietary fiber

*To moisten stale bread, place a wet paper towel
on top of bread and microwave until soft.*

Poundcake Poppy Seed Muffins

Veronica Coronado

2 c. flour
3 tsp. poppy seeds
1/2 tsp. salt
1/4 tsp. baking soda
1 c. sugar
3 T. margarine

4 egg whites; or 1/2 c.
    egg substitute
1 c. plain nonfat yogurt
1 tsp. vanilla
Nonstick vegetable
    cooking spray

1. In a small bowl, stir together flour, poppy seeds, salt and baking soda.
2. In a large bowl, cream together sugar and margarine.
3. Beat in eggs whites (or egg substitute).
4. Beat in yogurt and vanilla until well blended.
5. Stir in flour mixture until moistened thoroughly.
6. Spoon batter into muffin tins sprayed with cooking spray; bake at 400°F. for 15 to 20 minutes or until wooden pick inserted in center comes out clean.

Yield: 12 servings
Per Serving (1 muffin):
   177 cal, 3 gm fat, 4 gm pro, 33 gm carb, 0 mg chol, 171 mg sodium, 1 gm dietary fiber

Reduce baking temperature 25° to prevent
over-browning when cooking with honey.

Light Angel Biscuits

Patty Kirk, R.D.

1/2 c. warm water (105°
   to 115°)
1 T. honey
1 pkg. dry yeast
1 c. wholewheat flour
1/2 c. dry yellow cornmeal
1 tsp. baking powder
1/4 tsp. baking soda

1/4 tsp. salt
1 c. low-fat buttermilk
1/4 c. vegetable oil
2 to 2 1/4 c. all-purpose
   flour, divided
Nonstick vegetable cooking
   spray

1. Combine first 3 ingredients in a large bowl; let stand 5 minutes.
2. Add wholewheat flour and next 6 ingredients; beat at medium speed with electric mixer until well blended.
3. Gradually stir in 1 3/4 to 2 cups all-purpose flour until a soft dough forms.
4. Turn dough out onto a lightly floured surface. Knead until smooth and elastic (about 8 minutes); add remaining flour 1 tablespoon at a time, to prevent dough from sticking to hands. Cover dough. Let rest 10 minutes.
5. Roll dough to 1/2-inch thickness; cut into rounds with a 2 1/2-inch biscuit cutter.
6. Place biscuits on a baking sheet coated with cooking spray. Bake at 375°F. for 20 to 22 minutes or until lightly browned.

Yield: 20 biscuits
Per Serving (1 biscuit):
   110 cal, 3 gm fat, 3 gm pro, 18 gm carb, 0 mg chol, 71 mg sodium, 1 gm dietary fiber

A
Little
Something
Sweet

A Little Something Sweet

A Little Something Sweet

Fresh Blueberry Crunch   Mary Norsworthy

4 c. fresh blueberries
1 c. brown sugar, firmly
   packed
1/4 c. flour

3/4 c. oatmeal, dry
1/4 c. margarine, melted
Nonfat frozen yogurt (optional)

1. Place blueberries in a 2-quart baking dish and spread evenly.
2. Combine remaining ingredients; sprinkle over blueberries.
3. Bake at 350°F. for 45 minutes.
4. Serve warm with yogurt.

Yield: 10 servings
Per Serving:
   194 cal, 5 gm fat, 2 gm pro, 36 gm carb, 0 mg chol, 64 mg sodium, 2 gm dietary fiber

To make powdered sugar, blend 1 cup granulated sugar and 1 tablespoon cornstarch in the blender at medium speed for 2 minutes.

Apple Oat Crisp

Nutrition Staff

FRUIT:
3 sm. apples, cored &
    sliced
1/2 c. applesauce

1 1/2 tsp. lemon juice
1/2 tsp. lemon rind, grated
1 tsp. sugar
1/4 tsp. cinnamon

TOPPING:
1/3 c. oatmeal, dry
2 T. wholewheat flour
2 T. brown sugar, firmly
    packed

1/4 tsp. cinnamon
1 T. plus 1 tsp. diet
    margarine

1. In a medium non-aluminum bowl, combine all fruit ingredients; pour into an 8-inch square baking dish.
2. Prepare topping in a small bowl by combining oatmeal, flour, brown sugar and cinnamon.
3. Cut margarine into topping mixture with a pastry blender until crumbly.
4. Sprinkle topping evenly over apple mixture.
5. Bake at 350°F. for 35 to 40 minutes until apples are tender and topping is browned; serve hot.

Yield: 4 servings
Per Serving:
    165 cal, 3 gm fat, 2 gm pro, 39 gm carb, 0 mg chol, 53 mg sodium, 4 gm dietary fiber

To remove the white membrane from oranges, for fancy desserts or salads, soak them in boiling water for 5 minutes before you peel them.

Mini Fruit Pizza

Patty Kirk, R.D.

2 (1/2") slices of refrigerated sugar cookie dough;
or 2 lg. sugar cookies
1/4 c. low-fat cottage
cheese, creamed in
food processor
1 tsp. powdered sugar
1/8 tsp. vanilla

2 canned peach slices
in its own juice, drain-
ed & cut into strips
1 sm. kiwi fruit, peeled &
thinly sliced
2 tsp. reduced-sugar
apricot spread, melted

1. Cut 2 (1/2-inch) thick slices from dough; press each slice into a 4-inch circle on a baking sheet.
2. Bake at 350°F. for 10 minutes or until golden.
3. Cool 1 minute on pan and transfer to wire rack.
4. Combine next 3 ingredients in bowl; stir well.
5. Spread half of mixture on each cookie; top with peaches and kiwi fruit.
6. Brush with apricot spread; serve immediately.

Yield: 2 servings
Per Serving (1 pizza):
161 cal, 4 gm fat, 5 gm pro, 23 gm carb, 15 mg chol, 226 mg sodium, 1 gm dietary fiber

Fresh Fruit Tart

Jean Wisner, R.D.

1 (16 oz.) prepared sponge
cake shell
2 kiwi fruit, sliced
7 strawberries, sliced
1 peach, peeled & sliced
1/2 c. seedless red grapes,
cut in half

1/2 c. seedless green
grapes, cut in half
1 tsp. Fruit Fresh
2/3 c. apple jelly
Light Cool Whip (optional)

1. Arrange sliced fruit on sponge cake shell. (Begin with kiwi fruit, then strawberries, peach and grapes.)
2. Sprinkle all with Fruit Fresh.
3. Microwave apple jelly 1 1/2 minutes on defrost.
4. Brush fruit with softened jelly.
5. Serve with light Cool Whip if desired.

Yield: 8 servings
Per Serving:
300 cal, 8 gm fat, 3 gm pro, 55 gm carb, 0 mg chol, 171 mg sodium, 1 gm dietary fiber

Fresh Fruit with Almond Cream

Nutrition Staff

4 oz. Neufchatel cheese
2 T. honey
1 T. skim milk
1/2 tsp. almond extract

1 1/3 c. bananas, sliced
1 1/3 c. fresh blueberries
1 1/3 c. fresh strawberries

1. Combine first 4 ingredients in a food processor or blender; process until smooth. Cover and chill.
2. Combine bananas, blueberries and strawberries in a medium bowl; toss gently.
3. Spoon fruit mixture into individual serving bowls; top each with 1 tablespoon chilled cheese mixture. Serve immediately.

Yield: 8 servings
Per Serving (1/2 cup):
   113 cal, 4 gm fat, 2 gm pro, 19 gm carb, 11 mg chol, 61 mg sodium, 2 gm dietary fiber

Apple-Blueberry Stir-Fry

Veronica Coronado

2 T. sugar
1 tsp. cinnamon
1/4 tsp. nutmeg
Juice & grated peel of 2 lg. oranges

4 tart green apples
1 1/2 T. margarine
2 c. blueberries
6 T. low-calorie whipped topping (optional)

1. In a small bowl, mix sugar, cinnamon and nutmeg; set aside.
2. In a large bowl, mix orange juice and peel.
3. Peel, core and thinly slice apples; toss with juice.
4. Place a wok or skillet over medium heat; when wok is hot, add margarine.
5. When margarine is melted, add sugar mixture and cook, stirring constantly for about 1 minute.
6. Add apple mixture to wok and stir-fry until apples are soft (about 3 minutes); bring to boil, and boil for 1 minute.
7. Add blueberries and stir-fry until sauce is thickened; serve hot. Top with whipped topping if desired.

Yield: 6 servings
Per Serving:
   145 cal, 4 gm fat, 1 gm pro, 30 gm carb, 0 mg chol, 37 mg sodium, 3 gm dietary fiber

Banana Brownie Sundae

Gail Brosey

1 lg. banana, mashed
3/4 c. sugar
2 egg whites
1/4 c. nonfat dry powdered
   milk
1/2 c. low-fat buttermilk
1 tsp. vanilla
1/4 c. cocoa powder

1/2 tsp. baking soda
1 c. wholewheat flour
3 bananas, sliced
3 c. nonfat frozen vanilla
   yogurt
9 T. chocolate syrup
Nonstick vegetable
   cooking spray

1. Combine first 6 ingredients; beat until smooth.
2. Stir in cocoa powder, baking soda and flour.
3. Turn mixture into an 8-inch square pan sprayed with cooking spray.
4. Bake at 350°F. for 20 to 25 minutes.
5. Allow to cool and cut into 9 squares.
6. Top each with 1/3 of a banana, 1/3 cup yogurt and 1 tablespoon chocolate syrup.

Yield: 9 servings
Per Serving (1 square):
   287 cal, 1 gm fat, 8 gm pro, 68 gm carb, 3 mg chol, 146 mg sodium, 3 gm dietary fiber

Limit nuts in recipes...they are high in fat.

Hot Fudge Pudding Cake

Cindy Kleckner, R.D.

1 1/4 c. sugar, divided
1 c. flour
7 T. cocoa powder, divided
2 tsp. baking powder
1/4 tsp. salt
1/2 c. skim milk

1/3 c. margarine, melted
1 1/2 tsp. vanilla
1/2 c. brown sugar, firmly
   packed
1 1/4 c. hot water

1. In a medium mixing bowl, combine 3/4 cup sugar, flour, 3 tablespoons cocoa powder, baking powder and salt.
2. Blend in milk, melted margarine and vanilla; beat until smooth.
3. Pour batter into 8 or 9-inch square pan.
4. In a small bowl, combine remaining 1/2 cup sugar, brown sugar and remaining 4 tablespoons cocoa powder.
5. Sprinkle mixture evenly over batter.
6. Pour hot water over top; do not stir.
7. Bake at 350°F. for 40 minutes or until center is almost set.
8. Let stand 15 minutes.
9. Spoon into dessert dishes, spooning sauce from bottom of pan over top.
10. Garnish with light Cool Whip (optional).

Yield: 9 servings
Per Serving:
   276 cal, 7 gm fat, 2 gm pro, 52 gm carb, 0 mg chol, 258 mg sodium, 2 gm dietary fiber

Limit sweets to 1 to 2 servings per week for weight reduction and 3 to 4 per week for weight maintenance.

Chocolate Zucchini Cake

Veronica Coronado

1 1/2 c. sugar
6 T. margarine
1 tsp. vanilla
4 egg whites
2 1/2 c. flour
1/2 c. light sour cream
1/4 c. cocoa powder
1 tsp. baking soda

1/2 tsp. salt
1 to 2 med. zucchini (8 oz.),
    shredded (about 2 c.)
1/2 c. walnuts, chopped
2 T. powdered sugar
Nonstick vegetable
    cooking spray

1. Preheat oven to 350°F.
2. Spray a 13x9x2-inch baking pan with cooking spray and lightly flour.
3. In a large bowl, with mixer at low speed, beat sugar, margarine, vanilla and egg whites until blended.
4. Increase speed to high; beat until light and fluffy, about 5 minutes.
5. Reduce speed to low; add flour, sour cream, cocoa powder, baking soda and salt. Beat until blended, constantly scraping bowl.
6. Increase speed to medium; beat 1 minute, occasionally scraping bowl.
7. With a rubber spatula, fold in zucchini and walnuts (batter will be thick).
8. Spread batter evenly in pan.
9. Bake 40 to 45 minutes until wooden pick inserted in center of cake comes out clean; cool cake in pan on wire rack.
10. To serve, sprinkle with powdered sugar.

Yield: 16 servings
Per Serving:
   222 cal, 7 gm fat, 4 gm pro, 36 gm carb, 0 mg chol, 195 mg sodium, 1 gm dietary fiber

One typical piece of chocolate cake with frosting contains approximately 420 calories and 19 grams of fat.

Chocolate Cocoa Cake

Georgia Kostas, M.P.H., R.D.

1/2 c. skim milk
1 1/2 tsp. vinegar
1 c. water
7 T. margarine
6 T. cocoa powder
2 c. flour
2 c. sugar

1/2 c. egg substitute; or 4
   egg whites
2 T. baking powder
1 tsp. vanilla
Nonstick vegetable
   cooking spray

TOPPING:
6 T. margarine
6 T. skim milk
6 T. cocoa powder

1 tsp. vanilla
1 lb. box powdered sugar
1/4 c. unsalted pecans or
   walnuts, chopped

1. Preheat oven to 325°F.
2. Mix milk and vinegar together; set aside to sour.
3. Bring water, margarine and cocoa to a boil in a saucepan.
4. Mix flour and sugar in a bowl and blend in hot cocoa mixture.
5. Add egg substitute, sour milk, baking powder and vanilla until well mixed.
6. Bake 50 minutes in a 13x9x2-inch pan sprayed with cooking spray.
7. Five minutes before cake is done, melt margarine, milk, cocoa and vanilla together (topping ingredients).
8. Mix in powdered sugar.
9. Spread topping on cake immediately after removing cake from oven. Sprinkle nuts on top.

Yield: 24 servings
Per Serving:
   250 cal, 7 gm fat, 2 gm pro, 46 gm carb, 0 mg chol, 197 mg sodium, 1 gm dietary fiber

Keep apples, bananas, pears and other fruits from discoloring when cut up by coating them with orange juice or diluted lemon juice.

Chocolate Buttermilk Cake

Susan Hoobler

2 c. sugar
3 c. flour
6 T. cocoa powder
2 tsp. baking soda
1 tsp. salt

1 tsp. vanilla
1/4 c. vegetable oil
2 c. cold water
3/4 c. low-fat buttermilk

1. Preheat oven to 350°F.
2. Combine sugar, flour, cocoa powder, baking soda and salt.
3. Add remaining ingredients.
4. Pour into a small pan. Bake for 25 to 30 minutes.

Yield: 16 servings
Per Serving:
211 cal, 4 gm fat, 3 gm pro, 43 gm carb, 0 mg chol, 258 mg sodium, 1 gm dietary fiber

One gram of fat equals 9 calories.

Fruited Angel Ice

Cindy Wachtler, R.D.

1 angel food cake

1 1/2 c. sherbet (lemon, orange, pineapple), softened

SAUCE:

2 c. frozen unsweetened raspberries

2 c. frozen unsweetened strawberries

1/4 c. sugar

1/2 tsp. orange peel, grated

1 c. blueberries

1. With serrated knife, slice 1/2-inch from top of cake, keeping this piece intact.
2. Keeping 1/2-inch border on both sides and at bottom of cake, remove the center portion.
3. Using spoon, fill center of cake with sherbet, replace top, cover tightly and freeze until firm (2 to 3 hours).
4. Place slightly thawed raspberries and strawberries in food processor fitted with steel blade; process until smooth.
5. Add sugar and orange peel; blend.
6. Slice cake into 20 slices.
7. Pour 2 tablespoons of sauce on each slice; sprinkle with a tablespoon of blueberries.

Yield: 20 servings
Per Serving:
124 cal, 0 gm fat, 2 gm pro, 29 gm carb, 1 mg chol, 52 mg sodium, 1 gm dietary fiber

*For a sweet treat, choose angel food cake --
it has no cholesterol and no fat.*

Harvest Apple Cake
Cindy Wachtler, R.D.

4 c. unpeeled cooking apples,
  finely chopped
1/2 c. orange juice, divided
1 1/2 tsp. cinnamon
1 c. sugar
1/2 c. margarine, softened
1 (8 oz.) ctn. egg sub-
  stitute, thawed

1/4 c. skim milk
3 c. flour
2 tsp. baking powder
1/4 tsp. salt
2 1/2 tsp. vanilla
2 T. brown sugar
2 T. oatmeal, dry
Nonstick vegetable
  cooking spray

1. Combine apples, 1/4 cup orange juice and cinnamon in a bowl; stir well and set aside.
2. Cream sugar and margarine at medium speed with an electric mixer until light and fluffy, about 5 minutes.
3. Add egg substitute; beat 4 minutes at medium speed or until well blended.
4. Combine remaining 1/4 cup orange juice and milk; set aside.
5. Combine flour, baking powder and salt.
6. With mixer on low speed, add to creamed mixture alternately with milk mixture, beginning and ending with flour mixture; stir in vanilla.
7. Pour half of batter into a 10-inch tube pan coated with cooking spray; top with half of apple mixture.
8. Pour remaining batter into pan; top with remaining apple mixture, and sprinkle with brown sugar and oatmeal.
9. Bake at 350°F. for 1 hour and 10 minutes or until a wooden pick inserted in center comes out clean.
10. Cool in pan 10 minutes; remove from pan, and cool on a wire rack.

Yield: 16 servings
Per Serving:
215 cal, 6 gm fat, 4 gm pro, 37 gm carb, 0 mg chol, 174 mg sodium, 1 gm dietary fiber

Scrumptious Banana Streusel Cake

Veronica Coronado

6 T. margarine, divided
1/2 c. plus 1 c. flour
1/4 c. plus 1 c. sugar
Pinch of salt
2 tablespoons light brown
   sugar
4 egg whites
2 tsp. vanilla

1/3 c. skim milk
3 bananas, puréed
3/4 c. wholewheat flour
1 tsp. baking powder
1 tsp. baking soda
1/2 tsp. salt
Nonstick vegetable cooking
   spray

Streusel: Work 3 tablespoons chilled margarine into 1/2 cup white flour, 1/4 cup sugar and pinch of salt until it is the size of tiny peas, using a food processor or pastry blender. Set aside.

Cake:
1. Use mixer to cream 1 cup sugar, brown sugar and 3 tablespoons softened margarine until fluffy.
2. Add egg whites and mix until very fluffy (about 3 minutes).
3. Add vanilla, milk and banana; mix well to combine.
4. In a separate bowl, combine 1 cup white flour and 3/4 cup wholewheat flour, baking powder, baking soda and salt.
5. Add gradually to batter, mixing until very smooth.
6. Transfer batter to a 9-inch square pan that has been sprayed with cooking spray and lightly floured.
7. Sprinkle reserved streusel evenly over surface.
8. Bake at 350°F., about 45 minutes, until medium brown and toothpick inserted in center comes out clean.
9. Let cool before serving.

Yield: 16 servings
Per Serving:
   188 cal, 5 gm fat, 3 gm pro, 35 gm carb, 0 mg chol, 217 mg sodium, 1 gm dietary fiber

Fifteen graham cracker squares equal
1 cup of graham cracker crumbs.

Pumpkin Cheese Pie

Nutrition Staff

CRUST:

1 c. graham cracker crumbs

2 T. plus 2 tsp. diet margarine

FILLING:

2 eggs, separated
1/2 c. light brown sugar, firmly packed
1 c. part-skim ricotta cheese
1 c. canned pumpkin
2 T. lemon juice

1 tsp. lemon peel, grated
1 tsp. cinnamon
1/4 tsp. ginger
1/4 tsp. nutmeg
1/2 c. evaporated skimmed milk
2 T. cornstarch
1/8 tsp. salt

To Prepare Crust:

1. Preheat oven to 350°F.
2. In a bowl, combine graham cracker crumbs and margarine, mixing thoroughly.
3. Using back of a spoon, press crumb mixture over bottom and up sides of a 9-inch pie plate.
4. Bake until crisp and brown, 8 to 10 minutes.
5. Remove from oven to cool.

To Prepare Filling and Bake:

1. In a large mixing bowl, beat egg yolks with 5 tablespoons plus 1 teaspoon brown sugar until well mixed; add cheese, pumpkin, lemon juice, lemon peel and spices; stir to combine.
2. In a small bowl or measuring cup, combine milk and cornstarch, stirring to dissolve cornstarch.
3. Stir into pumpkin mixture.
4. In a medium bowl, using electric mixer on high speed, beat egg whites with salt until soft peaks form.
5. Beat in remaining 2 tablespoons plus 2 teaspoons sugar and continue beating until stiff peaks form.
6. Gently fold whites into pumpkin mixture.
7. Pour filling into cooled crust and bake at 350°F. for 35 to 40 minutes (or until knife test is clean).
8. Set on wire rack and let cool completely.

Yield: 8 servings
Per Serving:

219 cal, 7 gm fat, 8 gm pro, 36 gm carb, 71 mg chol, 257 mg sodium, 1 gm dietary fiber

Yogurt and Fruit Parfait

Cindy Kleckner, R.D.

1 c. plain nonfat yogurt
3/4 c. strawberries

1/4 c. blueberries

1. Spoon 1/4 of the yogurt into a parfait dish.
2. Top with 1/2 of the strawberries, followed with another layer of 1/4 yogurt.
3. Top with the blueberries, followed with another layer of 1/4 yogurt.
4. Top with remaining strawberries and yogurt.
5. Save 1 strawberry as garnish for the top.
6. Serve chilled.

Yield: 1 serving
Per Serving:
183 cal, <1 gm fat, 14 gm pro, 31 gm carb, 4 mg chol, 177 mg sodium, 4 gm dietary fiber

Fruit A La Yogurt

Cindy Kleckner, R.D.

1 banana
1 orange
1/2 c. strawberries

1 c. plain nonfat yogurt
1 T. honey
1 tsp. orange peel, grated

1. Cut fruit into bite-size pieces, combine and place in 2 fruit cups; set aside.
2. In a small bowl, combine yogurt, honey and orange peel until well blended.
3. Divide mixture in half; spoon on top of fruit.
4. Serve chilled.

Yield: 2 servings
Per Serving (1 cup):
191 cal, 0 gm fat, 8 gm pro, 42 gm carb, 2 mg chol, 88 mg sodium, 3 gm dietary fiber

Red Raspberry Mousse   Kathy Duran, R.D.

1 env. unflavored gelatin
1/4 c. cold water plus 1/2 c.
    tap water
1/3 c. sugar
3 c. fresh or frozen un-
    sweetened red rasp-
    berries

2 tsp. lemon juice
1 c. plain nonfat yogurt
1/2 c. evaporated skimmed
    milk
2 egg whites

1. Sprinkle gelatin over 1/4 cup cold water to soften for 15 minutes.
2. Bring sugar, raspberries and lemon juice to a boil with another 1/4 cup of water.
3. Simmer for 4 minutes, add gelatin mixture and stir 30 seconds.
4. Remove from heat, purée in food processor and strain out seeds.
5. Chill until cold, then stir in yogurt.
6. Beat milk and egg whites in separate bowls until stiff peaks are formed.
7. Fold into raspberry mixture and chill until set.

Yield: 6 servings
Per Serving:
117 cal, 0 gm fat, 6 gm pro, 24 gm carb, 2 mg chol, 72 gm sodium, 5 gm dietary fiber

Pumpkin Mousse   Susan Smith

1/4 c. cold water
1 env. plain gelatin
1 c. canned pumpkin,
    warmed

1 1/2 tsp. cinnamon or
    pumpkin spice
1 tsp. vanilla
1 pt. vanilla ice milk

1. Place water and gelatin in blender to soften for 5 minutes.
2. Add pumpkin, spice and vanilla. Blend well.
3. Gradually add ice milk.
4. Pour into 4 dessert dishes and chill until firm.

Yield: 4 servings
Per Serving:
122 cal, 3 gm fat, 5 gm pro, 20 carb, 9 mg chol, 55 mg sodium, 1 gm dietary fiber

Fluffy Tapioca Pudding

Patty Kirk, R. D.

1 egg white	2 c. skim milk
1/3 c. sugar	1 egg yolk
3 T. tapioca	1 tsp. vanilla

1. Beat egg white until foamy, gradually beat in half the sugar, and continue beating until mixture forms soft rounded peaks.
2. Mix tapioca, remaining sugar, skim milk and egg yolk in a saucepan; let stand 5 minutes.
3. Cook and stir tapioca mixture over medium heat until mixture comes to a boil
4. Gradually add to egg white mixture, stirring quickly just until blended.
5. Stir in vanilla and cool 20 minutes. Stir and serve warm or chilled.

Yield: 6 servings
Per Serving:
99 cal, 1 gm fat, 4 gm pro, 18 gm carb, 37 mg chol, 53 mg sodium, 0 gm dietary fiber

Pistachio Pineapple Pudding

Edna Ground

1 (20 oz.) can crushed pineapple in its own juice	1 3/4 c. light Cool Whip
1 (4 oz.) pkg. sugar-free instant pistachio pudding mix	1/3 c. walnuts, chopped (optional)

1. Mix together pineapple (undrained) and pudding.
2. Fold in Cool Whip and walnuts and serve.

Yield: 8 servings
Per Serving:
97 cal, 1 gm fat, 0 gm pro, 20 gm carb, 0 mg chol, 463 mg sodium, 1 gm dietary fiber

Holiday Gelatin Dessert

Kathy Duran, R.D.

1 c. orange juice
1 sm. pkg. fruit-flavored sugar-
    free Jello (orange, apricot,
    etc.)

1 c. low-fat buttermilk

1. Bring orange juice to a boil.
2. Add package of Jello to boiling juice and stir to dissolve.
3. Add buttermilk and blend well.
4. Pour into prepared gelatin mold; chill until firm.

Yield: 4 servings
Per Serving:
   59 cal, <1 gm fat, 4 gm pro, 10 gm carb, 1 mg chol, 145 mg sodium,
   0 gm dietary fiber

Frozen Peach Dream

Karen Angevine, R.D.

4 sm. peaches, quartered
    & peeled

3/4 c. skim milk
2 T. sugar

1. Chop peaches in a food processor.
2. Add milk and sugar and blend.
3. Place in a small ice cream maker and freeze according to manufacturer's directions.

Yield: 4 servings
Per Serving:
   69 cal, 0 gm fat, 2 gm pro, 15 gm carb, 1 mg chol, 23 mg sodium, 1 gm
   dietary fiber

Frozen Yogurt Treat

Cindy Kleckner, R.D.

2 (10 oz.) pkg. frozen
  strawberries, thawed
1 T. unflavored gelatin

2 c. plain nonfat yogurt
12 (3 oz.) paper cups

1. Drain strawberries; reserving liquid.
2. Place drained liquid in a saucepan and sprinkle with gelatin; cook over low heat, stirring constantly, until gelatin dissolves.
3. Mix strawberries, yogurt and gelatin mixture in a blender container until smooth.
4. Place paper cups on a tray or a baking pan; fill with blended mixture.
5. Cover cups with a sheet of foil.
6. Freeze until firm.

Yield: 12 servings
Per Serving:
  68 cal, 0 gm fat, 3 gm pro, 15 gm carb, 1 mg chol, 31 mg sodium, 1 gm dietary fiber

Frozen Fruit Dessert Salad

Susan Smith

3 bananas, mashed
1 (8 oz.) can crushed pineapple in its own juice,
  drained
1/2 c. maraschino cherries,
  cut in half
1/2 c. plain nonfat yogurt

3/4 c. sugar
2 T. lemon juice
1 1/2 c. light sour cream
1/4 c. pecans, chopped
1 or 2 drops red food
  coloring

1. Mix all ingredients together.
2. Pour into 9x9-inch glass dish and freeze.
3. Remove from freezer approximately 5 minutes before serving.
4. Cut into 9 squares and serve on lettuce leaf.

Yield: 9 servings
Per Serving:
  197 cal, 5 gm fat, 4 gm pro, 37 gm carb, 0 mg chol, 51 mg sodium, 1 gm dietary fiber

Oatmeal Raspberry Bars   Susan Costello

1/3 c. margarine
2/3 c. brown sugar, firmly
   packed
1 tsp. vanilla
1 c. oatmeal, dry
1 c. flour
1/2 tsp. baking soda

1/4 tsp. salt
1 (10 oz.) pkg. frozen
   unsweetened raspberries
2 T. sugar
2 T. cornstarch
1/4 tsp. almond extract

1. Place margarine in a 2-quart glass bowl; microwave at high for 10 seconds or until softened.
2. Add brown sugar; beat at high speed with an electric mixer for 5 minutes or until creamy.
3. Add vanilla; mix well.
4. Add oatmeal and next 3 ingredients, stirring until mixture resembles coarse meal.
5. Press 2 cups flour mixture in the bottom of an 8-inch square baking dish; set aside remaining flour mixture.
6. Microwave at high for 2 1/2 to 3 minutes or until crust looks puffed, rotating dish a half-turn after 1 1/2 minutes; set aside.
7. Microwave raspberries (in their package) at high for 2 to 2 1/2 minutes or until thawed.
8. Combine raspberries, sugar and cornstarch in a 2-cup glass measuring cup; microwave at high for 2 1/2 minutes or until thickened and bubbly, stirring after 1 1/2 minutes.
9. Stir in almond extract.
10. Spread raspberry mixture over crust; top with remaining flour mixture; microwave on high for 3 1/2 to 3 minutes and 45 seconds or until bubbly and top looks puffed, rotating dish a half-turn after 2 minutes.
11. Let cool.

Yield: 16 servings
Per Serving (1 bar):
     134 cal, 4 gm fat, 2 gm pro, 12 gm carb, 0 mg chol, 106 mg sodium, 2 gm dietary fiber

Chocolate Cookies

Gail Brosey

1/2 c. sugar
1/4 c. skim milk
1/4 c. egg substitute
1 tsp. vanilla (or for variation use 1/2 tsp. mint
extract)
1 c. oatmeal, finely ground*

3 T. cocoa powder
1/2 c. wholewheat flour
1 tsp. baking powder
Nonstick vegetable
cooking spray

1. Combine first 4 ingredients; stir until blended.
2. Mix in next 4 ingredients.
3. Let batter stand 10 minutes and drop by teaspoonfuls onto cookie
   sheet sprayed with cooking spray.
4. Bake at 350°F. for 7 minutes.
5. Store in a covered container in refrigerator.

*Grind oatmeal in food processor.

Yield: 32 cookies
Per Serving (1 cookie):
   31 cal, 0 gm fat, 1 gm pro, 7 gm carb, 0 mg chol, 19 mg sodium, 1 gm
   dietary fiber

*One small chocolate chip cookie contains
approximately 57 calories and 3 grams of fat.*

Raisin Oatmeal Cookies

Georgia Kostas, M.P.H., R. D.

1 c. wholewheat flour
1/2 tsp. baking soda
1/2 tsp. salt
1/4 tsp. cinnamon
1/8 tsp. ground cloves
1/8 tsp. nutmeg
1 1/2 c. oatmeal, dry
2 egg whites, slightly
    beaten

1/4 c. brown sugar
1/4 c. dates, chopped
1/3 c. oil
1/2 c. skim milk
1 tsp. vanilla
1 c. raisins
Nonstick vegetable
    cooking spray

1. Preheat oven to 350°F.
2. In a bowl, sift together flour, baking soda, salt, cinnamon, cloves and nutmeg; stir in oatmeal.
3. In a separate bowl, combine egg whites, brown sugar, dates, oil, skim milk, vanilla and raisins.
4. Add to flour mixture; mix well.
5. Drop batter a teaspoon at a time onto cookie sheet coated with cooking spray.
6. Bake 12 to 15 minutes depending on texture desired; shorter baking time results in a chewy soft cookie, the longer time in a crisp cookie.

Yield: 24 cookies
Per Serving (1 cookie):
    98 cal, 3 gm fat, 2 gm pro, 15 gm carb, 0 mg chol, 70 mg sodium, 2 gm dietary fiber

Cardinal Sundae Sauce   Patty Kirk, R.D.

1/2 c. frozen strawberry halves, thawed	1 tsp. cornstarch
1/2 c. frozen raspberries, thawed	1/4 tsp. lemon juice
	1 T. currant jelly

1. Drain strawberries and raspberries; reserve juice and set berries aside.
2. In saucepan, combine cornstarch and lemon juice with berry liquid.
3. Bring to a boil and simmer gently for 1 minute.
4. Stir in jelly until it melts.
5. Remove from heat; stir in berries.
6. Chill.
7. Serve over lime sherbet or flavor of your choice.

Yield: 8 servings
Per Serving (2 tablespoons):
39 cal, 0 gm fat, 0 gm pro, 10 gm carb, 0 mg chol, 0 mg sodium, 1 gm dietary fiber

Fine Foods for Giving

Fine Foods for Giving

Fine Foods for Giving

Banana Bread

Nutrition Staff

1 c. flour, sifted
1/2 c. wholewheat flour,
   sifted
1/2 c. sugar
2 tsp. baking powder
1 tsp. baking soda
1/4 tsp. salt
1 tsp. cinnamon

1 tsp. allspice
1/2 c. wheat germ
3 ripe bananas, mashed
1/2 c. low-fat buttermilk
3 T. vegetable oil
4 egg whites
Nonstick vegetable
   cooking spray

1. Stir together the flours, sugar, baking powder, baking soda, salt, cinnamon, allspice and wheat germ.
2. Add all remaining ingredients; stir until blended.
3. Place in loaf pan sprayed with cooking spray and bake at 350°F. for about 1 hour or until done.

Yield: 1 loaf (16 slices)
Per Serving (1 slice):
   125 cal, 3 gm fat, 4 gm pro, 22 gm carb, 0 mg chol, 156 mg sodium, 1 gm dietary fiber

The most critical time of exercise is during the cool-down or recovery, immediately after a very vigorous aerobic phase. To avoid any abrupt cardiovascular change, keep walking or moving around slowly for a minimum of 5 minutes after completing the exercise.

Crunchy Peanut Butter Fudge

Nutrition Staff

2/3 c. nonfat dry powdered
milk
1/4 c. chunky style peanut
butter
1/4 c. raisins, chopped

2 T. plus 2 tsp. frozen
unsweetened concen-
trated apple juice,
thawed
3/4 c. Rice Krispies

1. In a small bowl, combine powdered milk with peanut butter, blending thoroughly; stir in raisins and apple juice.
2. Add cereal and stir until combined.
3. Press mixture into an 8 x 3 1/2 x 2 1/2-inch nonstick loaf pan.
4. Refrigerate until firm, about 2 hours.
5. To serve, cut into 8 squares; store in refrigerator.

Yield: 8 squares
Per Serving (1 square):
118 cal, 4 gm fat, 6 gm pro, 16 gm carb, 2 mg chol, 124 mg sodium, 1 gm dietary fiber

Almond Clouds

Nutrition Staff

2 egg whites
1/3 c. sugar

1/3 c. almonds, toasted &
finely chopped
1/2 tsp. almond extract

1. Beat egg whites (at room temperature) in a medium bowl until soft peaks form.
2. Gradually add sugar, 1 tablespoon at a time, beating until soft peaks form.
3. Fold in almonds and extract.
4. Drop meringue by heaping teaspoonfuls 1 inch apart onto wax paper-lined cookie sheet.
5. Bake at 300°F. for 35 minutes.
6. Cool slightly on cookie sheet; remove gently from wax paper and cool completely on wire racks.

Yield: 42 cookies
Per Serving (1 cookie):
   14 cal, 1 gm fat, 0 gm pro, 2 gm carb, 0 mg chol, 3 mg sodium, 0 gm dietary fiber

Mexican Nibbles

Nutrition Staff

1 egg white
2 1/2 tsp. chili powder
1/2 tsp. cumin
1/4 tsp. garlic powder

3 c. Corn Chex cereal
Nonstick vegetable
cooking spray

1. Beat egg white at room temperature in a large bowl until foamy.
2. Combine next 3 ingredients in a small bowl; stir well and fold into egg white.
3. Add cereal; stir gently to coat pieces evenly.
4. Spread cereal mixture on a baking sheet coated with cooking spray.
5. Bake at 325°F. for 15 minutes, stirring every 5 minutes.
6. Let cereal mixture cool on baking sheet; store in an airtight container.

Yield: 3 cups
Per Serving (1/2 cup):
   62 cal, 0 gm fat, 2 gm pro, 14 gm carb, 0 mg chol, 177 mg sodium, 0 gm dietary fiber

Bean Soup Mix
Nutrition Staff

1 3/4 c. beans (any type:
  pinto, black, kidney,
  black-eye, northern,
  whole or split pea,
  barley, garbanzo, lg.
  or sm. lima)
1 lb. turkey ham, chopped

1 (15 oz.) can tomatoes,
  chopped
1 lg. onion, chopped
1 green bell pepper,
  chopped
1/2 tsp. minced garlic
3 qt. water

1. Wash beans, cover with water and soak 4 hours or overnight.
2. Drain beans.
3. Chop tomatoes, onion, and green pepper; put in a large heavy pot with beans and garlic. Add water.
4. Cook slowly at least 5 hours.
5. To prepare as a gift, put beans in a mason jar and attach recipe on a card.

Yield: 8 servings
Per Serving (1 cup):
  220 cal, 4 gm fat, 20 gm pro, 28 gm carb, 45 mg chol, 654 mg sodium, 7 gm dietary fiber

Strawberry Vinegar
Veronica Coronado

2 c. frozen unsweetened,
  sliced strawberries

1 c. white wine vinegar
2 tsp. sugar

1. Combine strawberries and vinegar in a bowl; cover and let stand at room temperature 24 hours, stirring occasionally.
2. Remove strawberries.
3. Stir in sugar and bring to a boil in a saucepan.
4. Remove from heat and let cool.

Yield: 16 servings
Per Serving (1 tablespoon):
  4 cal, 0 gm fat, 0 gm pro, 2 gm carb, 0 mg chol, 0 mg sodium, 10 gm dietary fiber

Spicy Cider Vinegar

Nutrition Staff

4 c. cider vinegar
1/4 c. onion, chopped
1/2 tsp. minced garlic

1/2 tsp. crushed red pepper
1/2 tsp. coarsely ground
pepper

1. In a 1-quart jar, place vinegar, onion, garlic, red pepper and pepper; cover and shake vigorously.
2. Set aside for 2 weeks, shaking occasionally.
3. Strain out seasonings; pour vinegar into bottles with tight-fitting covers.
4. May add a parsley sprig, if desired.
5. Use in salad dressings and marinade for meat or fish.

Yield: 4 cups
Per Serving (1 tablespoon):
  2 cal, 0 gm fat, 0 gm pro, 1 gm carb, 0 mg chol, 0 mg sodium, o gm dietary fiber

Salt-Free Seasoning Blend

Nutrition Staff

1/4 c. plus 2 T. onion
    powder
1 T. garlic powder
3 T. poultry seasoning
3 T. paprika

2 T. dry mustard
2 tsp. oregano
2 tsp. pepper
1 tsp. chili powder

1. Mix all ingredients together; store in an airtight container.
2. Pour mixture into a shaker and use on meat, poultry, and vegetables.

Yield: 50 servings
Per Serving (1 teaspoon):
  7 cal, 0 gm fat, 0 gm pro, 1 gm carb, 0 mg chol, 1 mg sodium, 0 gm dietary fiber

Spicy Mustard Sauce

Nutrition Staff

1 (2 oz.) can dry mustard
3/4 c. med. dry sherry
1/2 c. Dijon-style mustard

1/2 c. pommery cracked
   seed mustard

1. Place dry mustard in bowl of food processor.
2. Pulse the machine on and off while pouring the sherry through the feeder.
3. Continue processing until you have a smooth, thick paste; add more sherry if necessary.
4. Add the Dijon-style and pommery mustards.
5. Turn the machine on and off a few times; adjust the consistency with more sherry if needed to achieve a thick saucy quality.
6. Store in a covered glass jar in refrigerator for up to 2 months.
7. Label and decorate container.

Yield: 1 3/4 cups
Per Serving (1 tablespoon):
   29 cal, 1 gm fat, 1 gm pro, 1 gm carb, 0 mg chol, 112 mg sodium, 0 gm dietary fiber

Tarragon Mustard

Nutrition Staff

1/4 c. dry mustard
1/4 c. warm water
1/4 c. white wine
1/4 c. red wine vinegar

1 T. flour
1 3/4 tsp. crushed
   tarragon leaves
1 tsp. allspice

1. In a small bowl, combine mustard and water; set aside for 10 minutes for flavor to develop.
2. In a small saucepan, combine wine, vinegar, flour, tarragon, allspice and mustard mixture.
3. Bring to a boil, stirring constantly; cook and stir until thickened, about 2 minutes.
4. Pour into a small bowl; cover and refrigerate overnight.
5. Beat vigorously with a wire whisk until smooth.
6. Spoon into container with a tight-fitting lid; refrigerate.
7. Label and decorate container.
8. Use as salad dressing, vegetable dip, seasoning for chicken or fish.

Yield: 16 servings
Per Serving (1 tablespoon):
   14 cal, 1 gm fat, 1 gm pro, 1 gm carb, 0 mg chol, 0 mg sodium, 0 gm dietary fiber

Index

Sip It

Awesome Appetizers & Souper Soups

Tossed Temptations & Delightful Dressings

Fresh from the Garden

Poultry with Pizzaz

Sensational Seafood

Lean Ways with Beef, Pork & Veal

Meatless Meals

Mama Mía

Mexican Olé

Beginning the Day

Fresh from the Oven Breads & Muffins

A Little Something Sweet

Fine Foods for Giving

ORDER FORMS

WHAT'S COOKING AT THE COOPER CLINIC

==

WHAT'S COOKING AT THE COOPER CLINIC

Nutrition Department-Cooper Clinic, 12200 Preston Road,
Dallas, Texas 75230

Please send me _____ copies of **WHAT'S COOKING AT THE COOPER CLINIC** at $14.95 plus $3.75 shipping for each book. Texas residents add $1.23 tax. Enclosed is my check for $_____. (Make checks payable to "It's Cooking, Inc.")

Name_____

Address_____

City_____State_____Zip_____

....

WHAT'S COOKING AT THE COOPER CLINIC

Nutrition Department-Cooper Clinic, 12200 Preston Road,
Dallas, Texas 75230

Please send me _____ copies of **WHAT'S COOKING AT THE COOPER CLINIC** at $14.95 plus $3.75 shipping for each book. Texas residents add $1.23 tax. Enclosed is my check for $_____. (Make checks payable to "It's Cooking, Inc.")

Name_____

Address_____

City_____State_____Zip_____

Visa, MasterCard and American Express accepted.
For phone orders, call the Nutrition Department at
214-239-7223, ext. 161

ORDER FORMS
FOR ADDITIONAL PRODUCTS & SERVICES
FROM THE COOPER CLINIC
Clip and Mail Today!

===

Recipe Analysis

Nutrition Department-Cooper Clinic, 12200 Preston Road, Dallas, Texas 75230

Enclosed are _____ recipes that I would like analyzed by the Cooper Clinic at $15 each. My check for $_____ is attached. (Make checks to "Cooper Clinic".)

Name_____

Address_____

City_____State_____Zip_____

....

Computerized Diet Analysis

Nutrition Department-Cooper Clinic, 12200 Preston Road, Dallas, Texas 75230

I would like to have my diet analyzed for 26 nutrients and receive nutritional recommendations. Please send me the Nutrient Analysis form to record my intake. I will return the form with $37 payment. (Make checks payable to "Cooper Clinic".)

Name_____

Address_____

City_____State_____Zip_____

....

The Balancing Act for Weight Control

Nutrition Department-Cooper Clinic, 12200 Preston Road, Dallas, Texas 75230

Please send me _____ copies of **THE BALANCING ACT NUTRITION AND WEIGHT GUIDE** -- a step-by-step no-gimmick approach to weight loss reflecting the Cooper Clinic philosophy of health and fitness. Cost: $29.95 plus $3.50 shipping for each book. Texas residents add $2.47 tax. Enclosed is my check for $_____. (Make checks payable to "Cooper Clinic".)

Name_____

Address_____

City_____State_____Zip_____

Visa, MasterCard and American Express accepted. For phone orders, call the Nutrition Department at 214-239-7223, ext. 161

NUTRITION TIPS

Nutrition Department-Cooper Clinic, 12200 Preston Road,
Dallas, Texas 75230

Be current on various nutrition topics! We offer 11 brochures
and 1 booklet prepared by Cooper Clinic nutritionists.

PRICES: Brochures - $2.00 each
$1.00 each (11-49 brochures)
$.75 each (over 50 brochures)
Booklet - Healthy Eating & Weight Control -
$3.00 each
$2.50 each (20-49 booklets)
$2.00 each (over 50 booklets)

PLEASE INDICATE THE NUMBER
OF EACH YOU WISH TO ORDER.

Brochures:

_____Optimal Nutrition   _____Eating Out
_____Eating on the Run   _____Fast Foods
_____Cholesterol & Heart Disease _____Fiber
_____Sodium   _____Diabetes
_____Nutrition & Athletics   _____Digestive Disorders
_____Hypoglycemia

Booklet:

_____Healthy Eating & Weight Control

Brochures: Total Number_____   Total Cost $_____

Booklet: Total Number_____   Total Cost $_____

Texas residents add 8.25% tax   Tax $_____

Please send me the brochures and booklets I have indicated.
Enclosed is my check for $_____. (Make checks payable to
"Cooper Clinic".)

Name_____
Address_____
City_____State_____Zip_____

Visa, MasterCard and American Express accepted.
For phone orders, call the Nutrition Department at
214-239-7223, ext. 161

Nutrition Tips are copyrighted and may not be reprinted.

Fundraiser Cookbooks ...

while fairly new to parts of the United States, are a proven successful fundraiser for many different organizations nationwide. How successful? We have had groups earn from $500 to over $100,000 on a successful cookbook. Here is a partial list of types of groups and organizations that have produced a successful fundraiser cookbook.

•Nutrition Associations	•Elementary Schools
•Charitable Organizations	•Middle Schools
•Police Departments	•High Schools
•Corporate Employee Groups	•Hobby Clubs
•Centennial Celebrations	•Welcome Wagon
•Families	•Libraries
•Churches	•Historical Societies
•Civic Groups	•Bowling Associations
•Hospitals	•Professional Hockey
•Sororities	Team's Wives
•Fire Departments	•Hunters' Associations
•Alumni Organizations	•Conservation Groups
•PTA's	•Soccer Teams
•Cub Scouts	•Little League Baseball

- **Do you belong to these types of organizations?**
- **Could your organization use additional funds?**

If so, let us help you put together
your own personalized cookbook.

Please take a moment and fill out the order blank on the back of this page and we'll send you our complete cookbook planning guide.
Or, if you prefer, give us a call toll free 1-800-798-2635.

We hope you are enjoying using this cookbook and find it useful in your kitchen. This book was printed by the Jumbo Jack's Cookbook Company. If you are interested in having cookbooks printed for your organization, please write us for prices and details.

A cookbook is a good way for YOUR organization to make money.

If you are interested in more information, just tear out this page and mail it to us with your name and address, or just call us toll-free 1-800-798-2635.

Featuring the
3-ring binder -

the cookbook of
the 90's
as well as the
popular
spiral binder

Yes -- please send
me more information

Name_____

Organization_____

Address_____

City_____ State_____ Zip _____

Phone_____

NO MONEY
DOWN -
5 months
interest free

Or, if you prefer give Mike a call:
Toll free: 1-800-798-2635,
Collect: 1-712-563-2635
FAX: 1-712-563-3118

JUMBO JACK'S
COOKBOOKS
Box 247 • Audubon, Iowa 50025